Pastor

The Incredible Dream

Michael Terence
Publishing

First published in paperback by
Michael Terence Publishing in 2020
www.mtp.agency

barringtonlewis1@yahoo.co.uk

ISBN 9781800940659

Contents

1

Life in Little Bridge, Jamaica

Easter Monday and everyone hurried excitedly to churches, celebrations, parties and places of entertainment. Meanwhile, Ms Lizeth Josephine Evans and Mr Linton Lewis, both at the tender age of 21, welcomed the birth of their second child, a healthy, bouncing baby boy. What better name could have been bestowed on me as a baby boy born on Easter Monday, than the one specified by my dear beloved mother: Otis, Saint, Barrington, Lewis.

Otis is said to be of German, Greek, or English origin. In German and English, it's linked to prosperity, fortune, riches and wealth. For the Greeks, it means keen on hearing. Saint, of course, refers to a very virtuous, kind, or patient person, even acknowledged as holy or virtuous. Barrington stands for fair-haired which in North America means favourite or cherished. As it happens, my given names turned out to be somewhat appropriate. Someone must have known that one day I would become a Christian and even a Pastor.

I feel privileged to have been born into such a wonderful extended family with grandparents Mr Edward and Mrs Hilda, Aunties Lucia, Dora, Cherry and Vivienne; Uncles Busta, Roland, Clenert, Randolph and Tony; cousins Dawn, Sandra, Richard, Courtney, Kevin, Judy, Terence and Iyenda, not to mention my two brothers Albeno and Roxroy and my precious Mum, Lizeth. When they were younger, they had been one big happy household but by the time I was born, most of my aunties and uncles had moved out, although some of my older cousins would be there periodically. I also have five paternal siblings, three brothers and two sisters.

Given the fact that hospital births were not as prevalent as today in my community, the local midwife was the first point of reference, as she delivered the baby. I was told that I was a very cute and very fair to look at. That was the best Easter gift a mother could ever hope for, a new, healthy baby boy. Even though my mother felt exhausted she couldn't have been happier with her second child. There were new hopes and aspirations as this child entered the world. The Bible clearly states that "children are the heritage of the Lord and the fruit of the womb is His reward," as noted in (Psalm127 KJV, King James Version is the preferred version used in this book).

At the time of the birth of their second child, Mum and Dad were living together like Romeo and Juliet. However, it didn't take long before things went steadily downhill and in the end, it was best they separated.

I can clearly remember those days when everyone else went to school and I had to stay home with Mum because I was too young to go there. My ABC book was an obsession for me. I remember ripping it, making Mum very unhappy with me. I yearned to go to school. I really wanted to join my sibling and cousins there but I just wasn't old enough. It felt tough being the only child at home. On the other hand, I could enjoy the Caribbean sun, breeze and beauty. Wherever Mum went, she would take me along with her and admittedly, we did have fun. Sometimes we would enjoy some nice juicy mangoes to eat at home together.

Oh, how I wish those times would return but unfortunately,

I can never share those wonderful moments with my mum again until the Second Coming of Christ, those cherished moments. When the dead in Christ shall rise and we who are alive and remain shall be caught up to be with Him in the clouds where we will be with Him evermore, (1 Thessalonians 4: 16-18). The Angels of the Lord will put us back into our family groups, so I am confident that my mum and I will be together again, (Psalm 50: 5). I long for that day when we will spend some memorable time together.

I shall never forget my first day at school. Mum took me and we walked the long journey from Little Bridge to Springfield, approximately two and a half miles. I was so tired when I got to school it was unbelievable. Of course, Mum couldn't stay with me, she had to go back home but she assured me she would come back for me in the evening. My voice must have echoed and re-echoed all over the community as I screamed and cried my eyes out. I told the teachers that I wanted my mummy; please give me my mummy back! They tried to reassure me that she would be coming back at the end of the day and I should not cry so much. The teachers were kind and gentle, however, that did not give me any comfort at all; it was overwhelming, it was too much for me to comprehend. I thought I would never see my mum again.

I was the happiest boy in the world when she finally arrived in the evening. It had been the longest day of my life. I hugged my mum, I held onto her tightly as I did not want to lose her. I realized then that the best place for me was to be at home with my loving, caring, kind gentle mother. She reassured me that everything would be all right and that I needed to go to school so I could learn and become a productive person in society. As we continued going to school day after day, eventually it became easier for me.

I remember clearly the teachers holding my tiny hands and teaching me how to write and how to say my ABC. It was fun and I watched and admired the older children who were in a much higher class than myself. They could write so nicely while I was just trying to write, it was my first day so it was a bit tricky for me. However, I continued going until finally I started making friends and I began to love school. I had a great time playing with my friends there and soon I would ask my mum to send me to school because I really wanted to see my friends. I still keep up with some of them to this day but unfortunately, others have passed away. When we moved out of what we used to call the basic school, I went to all-age school, which is now a primary school. Evidently, the first day at an all-age school was a million times better than my first day at basic school, because I moved up with my friends.

We had great fun playing Karate and Kung Fu. I was one of the best at Kung Fu, so all my friends wanted me to be on their team, no one was happy playing against me. We also went down to the crocodile-infested pond to play. As children, we were just having fun and having a nice time not knowing how dangerous karate could be. One day, I kicked one of my classmates in his tummy so hard, he fell down crying uncontrollably. I felt so sorry for him and what I had done.

I was good at my work and I did enjoy my early days at school, with Mathematics and English as my favourite subjects. I looked forward to doing these two subjects along with all my other schoolwork. I was really quick at Mathematics and actually enjoyed it every time the teacher asked me to go to the board and work out a maths question. I used to go to the shops as a young boy to buy things for my mum. After the shopkeeper had served all the items, she would ask me to do the calculation in my head for all the stuff I'd bought. I'd just calculate them in my brain and give her the right answer. She found this quite fascinating.

My early days of going to the shops were quite enjoyable. I had an old motorbike tyre that I pushed in front of me as I ran. This was like a bicycle for me. I felt like I had my own bike as I ran all the way to the shop, got what I needed and came running back home with it. I was sent to the shop more often than my siblings and cousins. I remember buying flour, sugar, cornmeal and chicken back, among other things. I really enjoyed cooked dumplings and curry chicken back. Our national dish was ackee and saltfish, which went down nicely with some cornmeal dumplings or better still, white flour dumplings. My mum always made nice cornmeal, potatoes or another pudding.

The transition from Parottee All-Age School to Pondside in my second year, leaving my friends behind, felt particularly painful for me. The impact was cushioned somewhat by the fact that there were students at that school whom I already knew from my community and we had always played together. So, it wasn't an altogether new experience for me and helped make the transition easier than it would have otherwise been. God always makes a way out for you even when you cannot see the end from the beginning. Although I missed my friends dearly from my former school, I quickly learned to get on with it and move on. Life had taught me from very early that sometimes one has to move on.

That experience of transitioning from one school to another helped me in later years in my role as a pastor. The nature of my job could see me posted at one church for six months or six years. Then it would be time to move on and carry the memories of people that you have loved and grown to know for many years. This is very difficult but I guess looking back at my early years of moving from one place to another, that must have helped when the time came to leave one congregation, my parishioners and enter into unknown territories.

It was a bit tricky at first but I quickly settled down in my new school. I had to learn how to make new friends and to understand the new school environment because it was not a very big school. My new teachers seemed to understand that I was new there and they were patient and understanding which made my transition a lot easier. The head teacher's wife was my first teacher; she was a very kind and caring person. My new school reminded me of the church because we would sing choruses in the mornings. The Bible would be read to us and we would be encouraged to memorize passages from it and had our devotional every single morning. That set a good foundation for me in the Lord because the Bible says to train up a child in the way he should go and when he is old he will not depart from it (Proverbs 22: 6). I shall cherish those formative years forever because they gave me a foundation that none other could have given me.

I looked forward to going to school, not only to learn new things, new skills, new abilities and to meet new people but also for those songs and scriptures to know more about God. Indeed, from a young age, I loved the Lord and wanted to serve Him for the rest of my life. To me this was food, real food, I loved and enjoyed very much memorizing the scriptures. I was hungry for the word of God, really hungry for the word of God. The Bible says he that hungers and thirsts after the righteousness of God shall be filled (Matthew 5: 6). God also said that when you search for Me, you should search for Me with all your heart, your entire mind and all your soul. God declares that you will find Me (Jeremiah 29: 13). I remember God speaking to me from a young age; I must have been about six or seven years old when God impressed upon my heart to be a minister of religion. I remember clearly God giving me sermons to preach and I could remember those sermons because no one taught me them but God Himself. It is a bit unclear whether or not I shared those thoughts with my mum, however, like Mary I pondered those things in my heart (Luke 2: 19). I truly believed that the time would come when I would be preaching and teaching others about the love of God. This all started in my formative years, growing up in a little community tucked away in the lush village of Little Bridge District, in the parish of Saint Elizabeth, Jamaica, West Indies. I had fun growing up I really loved my family, community and my country. I loved the different activities that we had.

Some of the activities I enjoyed most were cricket, football, swimming, searching for mangoes and playing board games such as Draughts. In cricket, I was a fast bowler, good with the bat and not a bad fielder. We would play in the evening we got home from school or during the long summer holidays. The same was true of football and playing draughts. I loved football; I was neither the best player nor the worst, just somewhere right in the middle. I used to go to the pond, sea and lake to learn to swim. I learned from a very young age and had a good command of the ability to swim. We had such fun as children. When it was either mango or guinep season, we would go to the trees or I would pick bunches of guineps or nice, juicy fresh mangoes.

We had a massive greengage mango tree in our yard and I would climb up and sit in it, pledging to myself that I wouldn't climb back down until I had eaten at least 20 greengage mangoes. Sometimes we would swim all day and when we got hungry, we would go and pick fruit from the trees because we could not afford to buy bulla cake and bag juice to eat and drink. By default, we were choosing the healthier option but we neither knew nor appreciated what we were doing at the time. With hindsight one can say we were quite healthy growing up in the Caribbean community.

The community was very peaceful and everyone cared about each other. There were no killings and no guns, or very few. Some people, smoked tobaccos, ganja/marijuana and others smoked cigarettes. People have always drunk white rum and JB. However, back then, it was a totally different community from what it has become. We live in a world now that is a global village, it appears that everyone is materialistic, everybody wants to do more and be more than they can afford and that has caused the crime rate to rocket in recent years. When we were growing up things were different, we were satisfied with what we could afford and the simple things in life would give us pleasure.

Oh, how I long for those days. You could walk on the streets at any time of night and all one would have to be afraid of was a duppy, a malevolent spirit or ghost, but not of another human being waiting to rob and kill you. I remember the older ones telling us about duppy walking around in the community. When someone died, people would put a tape measure on their doors because they believed that the dead person or duppy could only count to two. Therefore, when they saw the tape measure, they would stay outside all night counting one, two until daylight, and then they would leave. Others would paint their rooms, move furniture around and even wear certain coloured clothes and underwear in order to confuse the dead person. Admittedly, those things were not true, the Bible says, the dead knows nothing, both their love and hate perish at death (Ecclesiastes 9:5,6, 10; Psalm 115:17).

The breath of life and the body makes up the soul as noted in (Geneses 2:7; Ecclesiastes 12:7; James 2:26; Job 27: 3; Ezekiel 18: 20) The breath of life plus the body makes up the soul, take away any element and life disappears. When a person dies they cannot come back to life until Christ's Second Coming (Job 14: 13, 14; 1 Thessalonians 4: 16- 18; and St John 5: 28, 29). What people see are the evil angels transforming in the image of their relatives and friends (2 Corinthians 11: 13- 15; 1 Samuels 28), not their loved ones.

In those days, we would often go to bed without remembering to close the door and no-one would come inside the house to try to rob us. Times were so peaceful back then in our little community. I pray to God every day that things might go back to where it was back then. Mum would leave the door unlocked when we were coming home in the night-time and we would just push to open it. We didn't need any keys because no-one would try to break into our houses, the community was one and we lived as one.

If you were coming home in the dark, you wouldn't be afraid of someone pouncing on you, to rob you or trying to kill you. However, you did have to be mindful of crocodiles on the road when you were coming home from the shops for instance. Crocodiles would often be seen crossing the road, going from one pond to the next trying to find food or greener pastures and if you stepped on one, it would not hesitate to attack you. The nights were so pitch-black, those who could afford it would walk with a torch, to see where they were going and avoid any incidents that could be fatal caused by a deadly crocodile's bite.

A crocodile will not attack you unless it is really hungry or has its loved ones, its little ones or even eggs, and it feels threatened by you and fears that you might strike first.

We couldn't afford to buy beef, mutton, chicken or fish every day, so we would content ourselves with gungo peas, red peas or red kidney beans, broad beans, runner beans, callaloo, cabbage, and chicken back. We ate this every day, not even realising how healthy it was to be consuming an almost meat-free diet. We thought that meat was the best. Admittedly, things have come full circle and now I appreciate the simple but healthy diets that we grew up on. As children, we would have fresh milk from the cows and goats. Some of our hot drinks included black coffee, lime bush tea, fever grass and mint to name a few. Hot drinks like Milo and Horlicks were a luxury; therefore we could not afford to drink those every day.

"Come, boy," my grandmother used to call to me. "Get some lime bush for me to make tea."

I would quickly go in the bush next to our house and get enough lime bushes to make tea for that day. Fresh lime bush tea with a spoon or two of golden, brown sugar went down really nicely with bread or fried dumplings. Most times the dumplings were baked or reheated overnight food; they tasted wonderful. In the mornings, we had different porridges. It could be cornmeal, or rarely, oatmeal, banana or some other porridge. These were all delicious with condensed milk. I still remember our two favourite brands of condensed milk. These porridges were yummy with a dash of nutmeg and other spices like cinnamon leaves.

Most times for lunch it would be fruit or when we could afford it, either bread or maybe a bulla cake from Brownman's shop. At times we all shared one bulla cake amongst a whole group of us. Each person wanted to get a taste of it. We had no electricity, television nor fridge. It was only later when I was about 13 that we had electricity and then we got a TV, a fridge and some of the other luxuries in life. When we were young children, most of us would go to Miss May's home to watch TV and our favourite show back then was Night Rider.

Once, I tried to find a space to look through the window and the curtains, I was so keen to see what was going on in this show and found myself battling against the mosquitoes that were on our heels. I was not very happy to know that at that time of the evening, we were outside giving them some blood but the choice between watching TV and being bitten by mosquitoes was clear. All we had was a black-and-white TV but we were so pleased to know that this technology existed and we could enjoy watching movies.

We felt so happy, on the way home, playing on the road and talking about what movies and programmes we had seen. These truly were the good old days. My childhood memory also extends to Hilltop, two kilometres each way, from my home to watch TV at Mrs Clara's house. By then we were watching Mr T, MacGyver and other movies, especially comedy ones. We enjoyed sitting on her veranda and watching TV through her window. Mr T was so strong! We appreciated the favour shown to us who were less fortunate and did not have a TV at the time. A lot of us would go over there to watch TV; it was like a movie house. What a contrast between then and what our children have got today. If they want, they can watch TV all day. We had two TV stations, which signed off at a certain time. After the 7 pm news, we would enjoy our movies while our mothers engaged in conversation, using it as a social gathering. We had no interest at all in what they were talking about, the movies were more than enough for us.

The mile and a half journey home from Hilltop to Little Bridge on beautiful moonlit nights were always welcome. It was comforting holding on to my mother's hand as we walked along the road. Admittedly, sometimes I was practically sleepwalking and it felt such a relief to finally get home. I was so sleepy I just wanted to jump into bed. However, we could not go to bed like that because we had been walking barefoot and running all over the place, stepping into all sorts of things. If we went straight to bed, we could have taken anything with us and the scent might not be that lovely, hence, we had to wash our feet at the standpipe properly before being allowed to lie down.

The sleep was sweet, we were so tired after playing all day at school, walking over three miles there and back and another three miles just to watch TV. When I jumped into bed it wasn't into the luxury of a king-size bed with only me sleeping in it, five of us had the luxury of sharing one double bed.

The nights were so dark, as children, we often felt too afraid to go and use the outside toilet. I would procrastinate and finally, when I fell asleep again because I'd been trying not to go outside to urinate, I would have a nice dream where I was using the toilet. Then I'd wake up and feel some warm liquid saturating me and know I was in big trouble because I had just wet the bed again. Some of us were a bit mischievous and would move another person who was sleeping into the wet section for them to be discovered in the morning and get in trouble because our mother would believe that he had wet the bed. It would not take long for my mum to find out the truth.

She was a very godly woman and every morning she

worshipped with us. She sang songs to let us know that it is in God we live and move and have our being. I remember her singing "Just Over the Mountain" and also "Holy Day Jehovah Rest" and "Master the Tempest is Raging." We sang these powerful hymns and Mama Yet really loved the Lord and wanted to give us a divine legacy. She would sing with all her heart and soul and I thought to myself that if I could sing like my mum, I would be a very good singer, indeed. Those songs stay with me even today. These were the formative years that taught us to place God at the centre of our lives because it is in Him we live and move and have our being (Acts 17: 28).

Not only did my mum teach us about God, but she also educated us about reality and life. For instance, she used Percy Sledge's songs "Take Time to Know Her" and "When a Man Loves a Woman" to help us when we were looking for a life partner. She also taught us songs like Shirley Caesar's "No Charge" showing us that we should appreciate our parents and what they have done for us in life. Referring us to the story in Kenny Rogers' song "Coward of the County" she educated us about the boy whose father was sentenced to life in prison. When he was just 10 years old, his father said to him, you don't have to fight to be a man.

She instilled enough confidence and courage in us to let us know that we could achieve what we set our minds to. She had a good education and wanted to be a teacher. However, when she applied for the job, they turned her down, apparently unfairly. She also applied to be a nurse and this was denied her, even though she had qualified in all the right subjects needed in those days. She had the potential to achieve a lot more academically and educationally. A strong believer in academia, she made sure that she gave us the best academic start in life.

My mother wanted us to achieve all that she was not privileged enough to attain. She taught us that it is not by might nor by power but by my spirit said the Lord of Hosts (Zachariah 4: 6). I can do all things through Christ who strengthens me (Philippians 4:13). This tenacity and my drive for moving forward and achieving and obtaining by the grace of God, I got that from my mother. She would not give up and she taught me not to give up but to keep pressing on.

Labi Siffre's wonderful song "Something Inside So Strong," says: 'the more you take my rights away from me, faster I will run, you can deny me, but something inside so strong and I know that I can make it but you do me wrong so wrong.'

So, when I get life's hard knocks, I tell myself the hotter the battle the sweeter the victory. Please don't believe that I am going to be deterred by difficulties or challenges, no, no, I won't by God's grace. Difficulties are only hurdles for me to surmount in the name of Jesus. I am not afraid of life's challenges because of that foundation given to me from God through my mother. Hence, if a person tries to stop me from achieving something, I'll push harder by God's grace. Inspiration said; "higher than the highest human thoughts can reach is God's ideal for his children, godliness God-likeness is God's ideal for his children," as held in the book (Education, pp. 18, 19). For us to achieve one has to work harder, dig deeper to achieve more by His grace and by His power. God will never leave you nor forsake you (Hebrews 13: 5 KJV).

My mum would tell us Bible stories and other motivational stories, which gave us the confidence that we could achieve whatever we set out to achieve by the grace of God. She would instil the word of God in us; as the Bible says, train up a child in the way he should go and when he is old, he will not depart from it (Proverbs 22: 6 KJV).

The teachings of those formative years stay with me even today and I will cherish that time spent with my mother. She taught me how to be a man, a person and a human being in the face of difficult and challenging circumstances. I went forward, knowing I had a purpose and a God-given mandate to make a mark, which will bless the world. The world should be a better place because I pass through it. She taught me that the sky is the limit and I should not settle for second best.

Most parents at that time were quite happy for their children to go to All- Age schools, which finished in year 9. The less fortunate pupils could leave school in year 7 or even earlier. My mum certainly did not want that for her children. She went beyond the call of duty to get at least a secondary school education for us, so we could have a fighting chance and establish a good foundation for the next step on the ladder of life. Things were really tough for my mother and I would have been more than content to continue going to Pondside All-Age School, like most of my friends. Children always want to leave school anyway and become an adult and learn the building trade, at least, that's what I believed. Fundamentally, my mum disagreed with me and insisted that I continued going to school over the age of 15. She decided that when I reached the secondary school age of 12, I would go to Black River Secondary School and that is what I did.

Meanwhile, between the ages of 10 to 12, along with two of my friends, I went to Salt Pond to help the men catch fish with a net. We would join them pulling on the rope attached to the net, which covered an area of approximately half a square mile, designed to catch fish, crocodile and whatever else was in its path. When the fishing net finally came to the shore, the men would release the crocodiles and other unwanted animals. The really big fish belonged to the owners but they were pleased to give us the smaller ones with a few complementary larger ones thrown in.

I was still a young child and we had to do this very early in the mornings. At about five o'clock, my friend came through the bush behind our house and called my name. I would be waiting for him and we'd set off to Salt Pond, collecting another friend on the way. The three of us went on foot through the bushes to a place with extremely dark water, called "Pass Water". This wasn't the only route to Salt Pond; we could have gone the long way, taking the road, a distance of approximately 3 miles each way. That journey was too long plus we would have been too tired on arrival and not have the strength to pull the net to shore. So, we always decided to take the perilous shortcut through "Pass Water".

The mornings were cold which made the water freezing. One can imagine the mud, the dark dirty water and a whole area infested with crocodiles. No-one wanted to be taken by a crocodile in those death-defying waters. The silence was deafening as our toes sank softly to the bottom and we navigated our way to the centre of the water. Only the occasional birdsong, the distant braying of donkeys, the mooing of cows and the crowing of a rooster, broke the silence.

Anything could have been lurking at the bottom of that dark water. Our aim was not to step on a crocodile or their young ones, hidden by them. When breeding, crocodiles are extremely vicious and protective of their young. If they suspect the young ones are in danger, they will kill you to protect them. It would be commendable if we as humans felt as protective and caring about our young ones and each other. As we walked deeper and deeper into the water, trying to get to the spot where we could come up safely on land, we still had a couple of smaller ponds to negotiate before reaching Salt Pond.

I used to acquire enough fish for my family and still have plenty to sell in the community, to whoever would patronize us. They would be satisfied with fish for dinner and we had the money needed for school. This gave me a level of independence, as a little boy from 10 to 12 years old. On our way back, we felt so hungry because we'd left home at 5 am without eating anything. Between 11 am and 1 pm, if there were mango trees or any other fruit trees in the bush then we would have a feast on those.

2

Secondary School

In 1986, the year I started at secondary school, a massive flood washed ashore in Jamaica on 6th June. The entertainers even have songs that they DJ about the sixth of the sixth 1986. It was very windy with torrential rain and cold. All the ponds overflowed their banks, the rain just kept coming, it was unbelievable the entire island of Jamaica was flooded which claimed 50 lives. It was under these conditions that we went to catch freshwater fish in our community.

We couldn't assume that fish would be the only things in the water, because the pond had overflowed its banks and everything that could swim or crawl was in there. We found different types of fish, turtles and crocodiles coming downstream towards us. Crocodiles cannot stay underwater for too long, they have to come up to get fresh air and warmth from the sunlight, so we saw their heads and teeth pushing up out of the water. We were still determined to go in and catch our much-loved fish, so we swam out from the bridge which gives our community its name, Little Bridge District and we had to be really good swimmers because the water was so heavy at the time, the bridge was almost breaking. The water that had always been below the height of the bridge was now rising and we wondered if the whole structure would finally disappear beneath it.

Under these conditions, my cousin, other family members and people from the community went into the water and I joined them. We swam across to set the net then we returned and started to beat the water as hard as possible whilst swimming back again towards the net. The fish swam away from us to escape and went straight into the net. We took those fish out and kept repeating the process.

It was on one of my journeys back that I realised I was swimming too close to the bridge and found the water pressure much stronger than I was used to. I struggled and tried my best to reach the roadside of the bridge and get out of the crocodile-infested water. Suddenly, the current pulled me towards the bridge trapped with all the debris and other stuff clogging up under the little bridge, if it dragged me under I would be completely unable to escape. I knew that if I got stuck under there for long, I would be unable to breathe and I was looking at a watery grave. On top of this, crocodiles were bound to be under the bridge, hiding from the noise that we were making, beating the water and they were ready to protect their young ones. Who knows what danger was lurking there?

Suddenly, my cousin Richard, who is 4 years older than me, appeared and pulled me to the bank. I was really happy and relieved to know that I escaped going under that bridge. Nevertheless, I was such a good swimmer so let's assume that nothing was under the bridge, I could easily have dived under the bridge again and still escaped a watery grave. In the meantime, I was very happy to be alive!

Things were really tough back in the day and I was getting very little assistance, if anything at all, from my dad, when the time came for me to start at Black River Secondary School that summer. It was nearly six miles each way from our home. We couldn't walk there barefooted as we did to Pondside School. My mum would have to find bus fare, lunch money, school fees, uniform and shoes. I wondered if she would ever be able to afford it because my older brother Albeno, who is approximately two years older than me, was already attending there. As I said, she had very little help from our father, how could she manage to send us both to secondary school until year 11? Would I drop out somewhere along the way for the lack of financial support? I wondered what would be the outcome.

I have vivid memories of children laughing at us because we were poor. I can never forget the words of one girl in particular, who said that Ms Lizeth can hardly find the money to buy flour so she can't afford to send two of her sons to Black River Secondary. My dear mum was determined to beat the odds and prove them all wrong.

So, clutching the recommendations letter from the head teacher of Pondside All-Age School, my mum took me to Black River Secondary School to make an application for me to start in the summer of 1986. This was a completely new experience for me. I had never been to Black River Secondary School. As a country boy, I was used to Parottee and Pondside, in my local community where I was brought up and where it was quite easy for me to navigate my way around. Also, I knew all the children because we went to the same church, funfair or just by generally playing games together.

However, Black River was the capital of St Elizabeth and this took it to another level. Pupils attended from all over Saint Elizabeth, one of the biggest parishes in Jamaica. This meant hundreds of students, more than the school could accommodate so they had two shifts, one in the morning, the other the afternoon. I was a shy boy. I remember going to the school with my mum supporting me as they showed us around. We spoke to the headteacher and to the people in admissions and I did the qualification exam.

I was delighted to know I had been accepted in the school. This opened my world and took things to a new place. I now had the potential to meet people from all over the parish and study at a higher level. The whole environment was different from what I was used to. This barefoot boy now had to wear shoes all the time, being a pupil of a school in the city. They provided us with information about what uniform to wear, the policies of the school and told me I would be on the morning shift that year. It was indeed with mixed feelings that I looked forward to starting in September. I had heard so many horror stories about students, who were unable to eat their lunches because the bigger boys would take the food away from them, punish them and bully them and how there was no-one to rescue them. In reality, this was not the case and I thoroughly enjoyed my time at the school, making friends whom I communicate with to this day.

Come September, my mum bought my khaki suit, with trousers and shirts made in the community by seamstresses and tailors. Sister Jones made the shirt and Uncle Randolph made the trousers. I wore my new uniform, shoes, bag and kit with pride. That first morning, I got up early, beaming with excitement as I waited for the taxi. The driver was kind enough to take us to the school gates and as soon as we walked inside, I realized how different everything was from my previous schools, where we only had one classroom. Here, they changed the classroom for each lesson, walking down long corridors to reach the next one.

I was quite pleased with my results at the end of the first year; out of over 36 students, I was the fourth highest. That was a real achievement for the first year at a new school, only two girls and one boy ahead of me. God be praised! I enjoyed PE and football at my new school as well. Another bonus was lunch, a patty and coco bread with a small box drink. I had a good appetite, so I really looked forward to lunchtime. This was just before the introduction of Nutribun and milk, which quickly took over. Some children were too proud to buy it since it carried a stigma that you were poor, so I took extras home with me and even the teachers did the same.

In year 8, I was asked to serve as Form Captain for my class, which I accepted, with great pride. By now I had changed to the evening shift at school, which was much, more flexible for me. The morning shift meant you couldn't do much before or after school but the evening one gave me greater independence and a chance to become more creative with my time.

Very early some mornings, I would join my cousin, uncle, brother and others going to the lake to catch fish, crayfish and shrimps. Sometimes my older brother and I went together to the "Naga Pond" to check our pots and see how many fish we had caught overnight. We all knew where we had left our fishing pots and we'd go with new baits, pull the fishing pots up, put all the fish in our bags and replenish the pots with new baits.

That water was very dark and dirty and it was also infested with crocodiles so we were taking chances going into it. In the morning just before sunrise, it was extremely cold and black as midnight so we had no idea what was underneath as we stepped into the pond. Sometimes we beat the surface of the water with our hands, hoping that if there were any crocodiles they would swim away, frightened we were coming to hunt for them; that was our one method of escape. Nevertheless, our hearts were always pounding because we weren't sure if the crocodiles had their young ones in the path where we were treading and as we know, they will kill you to save their babies, so we could only hope and pray we weren't about to be killed and possibly eaten by crocodiles as breakfast in black, cold, dirty water in the cool of the morning.

After making a good catch, we put the fish on strings and set off to sell it in the community. We used the money raised to buy food and to pay for us to go to school for the rest of the week, or at least for a couple of days, according to how much we got. After selling our fish, we returned home, had a quick breakfast and set off for the evening shift at school which started at 1.10 pm and finished at about 5 pm.

On other occasions, I went with my cousin and uncle to a different pond to catch crayfish. Fortunately for me, in years 8, 9 and 11 I was on the evening shift. This gave me many opportunities to go out early in the mornings to catch crayfish and sell them to vendors coming to our community specifically to buy them. These vendors would then sell them on in Kingston or other major areas. Again, we would go in the water very early in the morning but even though the entire area of Saint Elizabeth was rife with crocodiles, being not far from the Black River, I wasn't as afraid as I was in the Naga Pond. This water was just a running stream and we placed our pots in it then stayed generally on the bank.

All of this fishing activity produced sufficient income for me to continue at school. No-one knew what I had done before coming to lessons. I would be so tired at the end of school I couldn't do any further study when I got home. I knew I had to go back to the pond early in the morning to catch more fish. I quickly mastered this art and was really enjoying it day by day. I looked forward to it because it gave me a level of independence that I would never have had. My mum did not have to give me money anymore to go to school because I had enough to pay for it myself and to buy food to eat. This level of independence was a real blessing to me.

3

Commitment to God

I was in Year 8 at Black River Secondary School when a big tent was pitched in the Newtown community. This was done by the Seventh-day Adventist Church in Saint Elizabeth; in fact, all the churches were involved in this massive campaign. Buses took people from different areas of the parish and we would all descend on Newtown's green, leafy grass. I remember that tent so clearly and the bus coming into our community with us ready to jump on it, to be taken to the campaign centre at Newtown.

Every night when the bus came to pick us up, I would be eagerly waiting at a place called Lane Mouth, not far from my house. Since I was technically an adolescent at this time, I did not only go there for the good gospel singing and the challenging preaching but also to see and interact with the opposite sex of my generation. The bus that took us from our community to the campaign centre was called 'Fowl Roosts' because it was such an old bus and not in the best condition. However, we were delighted just to get standing-room on it because when it was full, some people would be left behind.

As children, we were taught to stand on the bus and allow others to sit down, particularly older people to whom we should always show respect. On arrival at the campaign centre, the standing passengers jumped off first and we set off to explore, walking around to see whom we could meet. We tried not to go in the tent for too long but be near enough for the finishing of the church service so we could be sure of the ride back home.

At that time of night, Black River and other communities would be ghost towns with no other transportation available. We made sure not to miss our bus and get left behind in the dark.

People would come from all over, especially to enjoy what was for sale from stalls at the side of the tent. We had money with us to buy peanuts. I remember one of my friends buying jerk pork and gave me a taste. I knew it was unhealthy for me as a 13-year old as held in (Deuteronomy 14 and Liviticus11). We saw many of our schoolmates at the campaign and had such a grand time. They had the best musicians, a very good speaker and loud music.

Years earlier, I told my mum that I wanted to get baptized and she told me clearly that she would not allow it until I was 12 years old. The reasoning behind this was that she was responsible for my sins; if anything happened to me, God forbid, then it would be her responsibility and not mine for my soul's salvation. From that day on, I promised myself that when I turned 12 years old, I would get baptized and become a committed member of the church and a Christian person.

However, age 12 came and went and I did not get baptized. Now I had turned 13, I found myself interested in what was being preached. By listening to the word of God, the spirit of God was working on my heart. The Bible states clearly that faith comes by hearing the word of God (Romans 10: 17). It is the word of God that brings faith to a dead soul. I could feel something springing up because of the working of the Spirit of God in my life.

One night the preacher made an appeal. I could not resist the power of the Holy Spirit and I went down to the altar. When the Bible workers gave me the decision card, I ticked on it that

I would like to get baptized and surrender my life to Jesus Christ. I also stated that I would like to be a committed Christian and receive visits from a Bible Instructor or the pastor. I remember Elder McCrae came to my house while they were visiting in the community.

When they came to my house, I was the only person out of all my brothers and cousins who had signed up for baptism on the form. They asked me if I would like to get baptized, I was quick to say yes. Approximately seven years earlier I had wanted to give my life to Christ in baptism. When they asked my mum, she immediately gave her consent, remembering her promise to me that when I turned 12, I was free to get baptized according to my wishes.

The Bible workers then left the house; the first baptism was on the Sabbath. However, I had decided that I would get baptized on Sunday night, the second baptism of the campaign. My mum taught us how to wash, cook, iron clothes and clean. That Sunday morning of the baptism I had finished washing my clothes and was just hanging them out on the line. My younger brother, Roxroy, was throwing stones around. I wasn't paying any attention to what he was doing because I was so busy hanging out my clothes and thinking about how I was going to get baptized that night and be a free person in Jesus Christ. For whom the Son has set free, Hallelujah is free indeed: (John 8: 36). The word of God declares that if any man is in Christ, he is a new creature all things are passed away and behold all things become new: (1 Corinthians 5:17).

Suddenly something hit me hard in the face. Stunned, I turned to see what had happened. One of the stones my brother was throwing had struck me above my eye and in a matter of minutes; it had swollen as big as my fist. This was a terrible disappointment for me, as a young teenager, how could I get baptized at this tender age with a bump on my eyes as big as my fist? Surely, my friends would laugh at me, everyone who looked at it would make fun of me. I decided then and there to wait for another baptism; I wasn't going to get baptized that night, I was unwell.

When the Bible workers came to my house to confirm everything was fine for my baptism and to remind me of the things that I needed to take with me, I told them that unfortunately, I could not go through with it. I would make another date because I knew they had several baptisms planned. The Bible instructor understood immediately what was going on and told me that this was the plan of the enemy, the adversary wanted to stop me from getting baptized and that's why this incident had happened to me. They encouraged me to give God the glory and get baptized that night. This was a hard thing for me, life is challenging enough in your early teens, to have this against me on my big night was tough. However, I decided in my heart that it didn't matter what had happened, I was going to be baptized that night.

That evening, after I had enjoyed a delicious Sunday dinner, my mother prepared my clothes for the baptism. I had everything ready, my change of clothes, the ones I would be wearing to the baptismal site and my little bag with everything in it. My mum was coming with me for moral support. My clothes were well pressed, well cleaned, well put together. My mum told me that if I was going to be baptized, I had to speak to my brother because we hadn't been on speaking terms. Of course, I gave in and did it.

As we went to Lane Mouth that day, I felt lighter; I felt the joy of the Lord, the peace of the Lord. The Bible declares that great peace have they that love thy law and nothing shall offend them (Psalm 119:165). I felt that I couldn't be offended by anything at all, I felt unmovable, always abounding in truth: (1 Corinthians 15: 58). I felt that God was with me, then who can be against me: (Romans 8: 31). I was in a totally different world as I went to meet the bus, this one was called 'Fowl Roost', note, it wasn't the newest bus in town.

God brought the bus safely to us. We heard the tooting of its horn down the road, telling us to get ready. I gladly jumped aboard, with my mum and the rest of my relatives and everyone else who was coming to the campaign that night. I certainly wasn't jesting that night; I certainly wasn't hanging out with the guys that night; I was a changed young man who had decided to take his baptismal pledge seriously. It was now, with the world behind me and the cross before me, no turning back, praise the Lord, no turning back.

The atmosphere was pure and holy, I could almost see and hear the angels travelling with us on the bus that night. It was peaceful, it was calm, and the Spirit of God was with us.

As soon as we arrived at the campaign, I went straight into the tent and listened to the preaching. When it came to the time for baptism, I would be telling a lie if I said there was no form of anxiety. It was a very emotional experience for me, a one in a million decision; I was about to be married to Jesus. He is the one who has always loved me and done so much for me, the one who has spared my life, time and time again (John 3: 16). He said come unto me you who labour and are heavy laden and I will give you rest, (Matthew 11: 28- 30). He said I love you with an everlasting love and with loving-kindness I have drawn you (Jeremiah 31: 3). He is my Lord he is my saviour He is my King (Revelation 19:13,16; Luke 2: 11).

When I entered the baptismal pool, it felt a bit cold, being a February night. Walking up to the pool felt really emotional. So many of us were getting baptized that night therefore there was more than one pastor in the pool (Pastors Reid and Bowers). When I got up from my seat, I felt the Angels surrounding me, the heavenly atmosphere, it was totally awesome.

As I climbed up into the baptismal pool it was clear that there was rejoicing in heaven because another sinner had come home (Luke 15: 7). I went to the pool and the deacon took my hand. I went down into the pool and the pastor held my hands, and then stretched his hand to heaven.

"Otis Lewis," he said. "Based on the profession of your faith, as a minister of the gospel, I now baptize you in the name of the Father, in the name of the Son and in the name of the blessed Holy Spirit." Paradoxically, I would become a pastor and use the same words to baptise others.

The preacher then submerged me in the pool until I was completely underwater. I was not petrified; I wasn't afraid of water because I was so used to water already. I've been even swimming with crocodiles so this was a pleasure for me.

As I rose up out of the water, straight away I felt different, I felt free, I felt the Spirit of God as I had never felt Him before. I felt that if anything should happen to me all was well because my life was hid with Christ in God (Colossians 3: 3). Evidently, I made my calling and election sure (2 Peter 1: 10). I could shout with the old Negro spiritual: Free at last, thank God I'm free at last.

I remember clearly climbing out of the pool, as I was guided out, I knew that God had given me a brand-new experience. I was rejoicing, I was praising God with my newfound faith and my new experience in God. I went to the changing room and my mum was right there waiting for me.

After changing into my new clothes, we went to find my Aunt Lucy who had just arrived from America, where she had been living for the past 13 years. This was her first time back and she and her husband had come to Jamaica for a holiday. She was a Seventh-day Adventist Christian and made a point of visiting the tent, even though suffering from jet lag. We had really nice clothes to wear courtesy of her, not only on this occasion but she used to send barrels to us with food, clothing, toiletries and other necessities. My aunty made sure we never felt ashamed of our appearance and that we looked as good as anyone else in the community. To this day I appreciate what my Aunt did for the entire family and me. May the good Lord continue to bless her and keep her well.

When the meeting was over, we all lined up to go on the bus and I entered it as a new person. That bus which would take us home, I now thought of as a fiery chariot taking us to our heavenly home (2 Kings 2: 11). Many of us who got baptized that night by God's grace we are still serving God in spirit and in truth today (John 4:24).

A lot of the young people I knew at that time, said they would give those of us who got baptized two weeks, maximum two months, to turn away from following God. It was believed that a young person would not be capable of holding out and continuing to be a Christian. That's why some people believed you should only get baptized when you're much older but that's not good at all, because if the truth were told the young can die as well as the old. This suggests that we need to surrender our lives to Christ before death strikes. The Bible says there is no repentance in the grave so when a person dies, they can't accept

Christ again (Ecclesiastes 9: 5, 6 & 10; Ecclesiastes 12: 1- 8; Hebrews 9: 27). We have to accept Him before we die, while the blood is still running warm our veins. I could not keep myself but I was convinced that God would keep me because the word of God declares that He is able to keep me against that day (2 Timothy 1: 12) and I will keep him in peace whose minds are stayed on the (Isaiah 26: 3).

This inspired me to put all my trust and confidence in God, therefore 32 years later I am still serving God. It is neither by might nor by power but by my Spirit said the Lord of Host (Zachariah 4: 6). For this I can take absolutely no credit because the word of God declares that it is in Him we move and live and have our being (Acts 17: 28), Christ in you the hope of glory (Colossians 1: 27).

These are some of the scriptures, which have given me strength for 32 years to hold onto my faith in God. I would be lying if I say to you that I have been perfect, I have made blunders but God has been good to me; He doesn't treat me as I deserve, otherwise, I would not be here now. Praise the Lord for His goodness and His mercies that are new every morning (Lamentations 3: 22, 23). You can believe in Him too, He will keep you by His grace (Acts 20: 32).

I have made mistakes that I have regretted and I'm deeply sorry for; it's not about being perfect why am I rejoicing in God but it's about God's loving-kindness and God's ability to forgive you, even when you have wronged Him (Psalm103: 12; 1 John 1: 9 Micah 7:18,19; Isaiah 1: 18). When you have gone astray He says oh backsliding Israel I am married unto you (Jeremiah 3: 6) and (2 Corinthians 11: 2). The love of God that sustained me for 32 years (2 Corinthians 5:14), as for me and my house we will serve the Lord (Joshua 24:15); if I live for another 32 years or more, I will still serve the Lord. God is good, He has done so much for me, more than I can ever think or imagine (Ephesians 3: 20), glory, power, majesty, might, thanksgiving both now and forevermore be unto Jesus Christ our Lord and Saviour then (Revelation 7: 12).

I was now a fully-fledged member of the Seventh-day Adventist Church, which gave me great joy. I was happy to be a member with full rights and responsibilities. Of course, there were challenges and obstacles to overcome. I was really quiet and shy; I was arguably the quietest young boy in the whole community. When I found myself in a big crowd I wouldn't speak, I would keep quiet and just listen to everyone and observe. Some people called me "a snake in the grass." Being a baptized member of the church posed unique challenges, in that I would now need to take part in the church, possibly go up on the pulpit and do or say something in the church. I was so shy I could not entertain the thought of going up in church and saying or doing anything in front of a congregation. When I got a bit older, I literally hid from Bible class because they would ask me to stand up and answer questions or read the Bible in front of everyone. I did not want to do it, so I never went back to church until Bible class was finished.

One day, to my surprise, I was asked to be a young deacon or usher, even though I didn't want to go upfront. After all, I'm not the type of person who would like to be upfront at all doing anything in the church because I was so quiet and so shy. As it happens, it wasn't very difficult being an usher because all I had to do was go around and collect the offering and hope they wouldn't ask me to pray at the end of our collection.

This year turned out to be a very important one for us, not only because I was now a baptized member of the church but also because we connected electricity in our house for the first time. We were blessed with a fridge and colour television to call our own so no more going to neighbours' houses anymore to watch TV. My two favourite shows were MacGyver and Mission Impossible. I looked forward to watching these movies now we had our own television. My mum utilized the fridge by selling box drinks and bag juices, among other things, at Pondside All-Age School so she could make a profit to help send us to school. Unfortunately, some of her box drinks and other snacks would go missing from time to time.

4

Hurricane Gilbert, The Storm of My Life

Approximately seven months after my baptism, Jamaica suffered one of the worst hurricanes ever seen. September 1988 and the hurricane season arrived in the Caribbean. We braced ourselves but at first, nothing happened. Our two radio stations RJR and JBC were constantly at our ears as we followed the news that Gilbert was about to descend on Jamaica in all its fury. I remember everyone making plans, sealing up our houses, getting stocked up with non-perishable foods and lots of candles because we were told that the power would go out and we'd have no water. We needed to know where our nearest disaster checkpoint was because if our house disappeared, that's where we had to flee to. People who were living in flood-prone areas were commanded to leave their houses and to go to their nearest shelter, which could be the local school or a church until the storm passed.

While Gilbert was threatening as a physical storm, another storm blowing in my life, here rages a storm between good and evil, the great controversy. Christ had just taken over my life and the enemy was threatening to blow in one of the greatest storms to try and take over my life from Christ, but I thank God that my life was hidden with Christ in God (Colossians 3: 3). Jesus said that he would never leave me nor forsake me (Hebrew 13: 5), so I had all the assurance that under His wings I was safely abiding though the night deepens and tempests are wild. I know He will keep me for he has redeemed me and I am his child, Ira Sankey composed this hymn.

I went to bed that night knowing the storm would be coming at us from the east. It would hit Portland, Saint Thomas and Kingston, head down to Catherine, Clarendon and Manchester before tearing into our area of Saint Elizabeth. Although our house was fairly new and made from bricks, unlike many others in the community, which were mostly wood, we were still petrified. I witnessed the thunder and lightning and I prayed to God, please Lord protect your child from this storm; protect us all in Jamaica from this storm.

Gilbert came in over the horizon and fortunately for us, a mountain and a big hill stood in its way. The hurricane had to pass Malvern Mountain and Pondside Hill before hitting our little community. We were in the valley and when the storm hit the mountain, we hoped it would not be able to dip so quickly. By then the hurricane was travelling at over 125 miles an hour and had risen to a category 5 storm. Malvern Mountain is the same mountain we looked at each morning to see the sunrise and judge when it was going to rain. We knew the weather forecast with one glance at it.

Although there is no Malvern Mountain in the Bible, God told us about a Hill; the Psalmist David says, I will lift up mine eyes unto the Hills from whence cometh my help, my help comes from the creator of heaven and earth (Psalms 121). God is the creator of heaven and earth. He is the one who gives us safety and protection from the storm. So, when I looked at Malvern Mountain, I was actually looking to the Hills from whence comes my help. He is the creator of heaven and earth, He created all things and by Him, all things exist (Genesis 1: 1;

Colossians 1: 16 - 20; Revelation 14: 6, 7).

Most people were glued to the two radio stations, RGR and JBC. We now had our own television set and electricity and watched the TV while listening to the radio at the same time, following the hurricane to see what would happen.

As the hurricane entered the mountain, I could see the trees shaking violently, moving back and forth, some uprooted altogether. Some people lost their roofs, others their entire houses. Hurricane Gilbert stormed towards our house at a speed of over 125 miles an hour. It was always called the New House, because my grandparents, on returning from the United Kingdom, had built a nice concrete brick house, the first of its kind in the community, the newest and the biggest. That was the house in which I was born. Would the new house be able to stand against a new storm, a new hurricane called Gilbert? The test was on for all to see. Gilbert ran like Usain Bolt towards our new house. I peeped through the window and saw this storm in all its fury coming down towards us. While our prayers were going up, the storm was coming down, with thunder and lightning dancing across the sky and a deluge of rain. It was an experience that I never want to have again. Finally, it hit the house where we were.

I crouched in terror as Gilbert tried to move our house from where it stood but the house was planted on a rock (Matthew 7:24- 27), thank God, it was unmovable. Admittedly, it shattered some of the zinc on the roof and caused a leak but this was nothing short of a miracle considering the disaster that we heard about in the east before it got down to the Southwest of Jamaica in Saint Elizabeth. We give God thanks and praise and glory and honour for He is worthy to be praised from the rising of the sun to the setting of the same (Psalms 113).

When we realized that our house was still standing after the storm, we knew it was a miracle indeed from God. There was no electricity and no water in the pipes but we didn't find it very difficult to go back to our lamps, the good old, home-sweet-home lampshades and kerosene oil because we were well prepared for a disaster like this. We had used kerosene oil and our old-fashioned lamps for many years before getting electricity. We had to consume the meats, drinks and milk from the fridge as quickly as possible. My mum was working at the school, selling drinks, juices, and other snacks. It was like Christmas had come early for us children because the fridge and freezer were full and we had all the box drinks, milk and eggnog that we could drink.

It certainly wasn't all doom and gloom because with the hurricane came a whole lot of fish in the water, as if they had been washed out from where they'd been hiding for years. We went out catching fish with our nets, as usual braving the crocodiles and made a good sale as well as enjoying a delicious warm fish tea at a time when the weather was cold and wet.

Also, at that time, we were doing some work for a lawyer who lived on Crane Road. I went there shortly after the hurricane and found his house was intact, as were those of his neighbours. We used to sleep over at his house occasionally, to take care of it as well as looking after the yard and in return, he gave us some money. We would feel so happy because we needed that money to help us through the days. Thank God the hurricane wasn't as bad as it could have been and working with this lawyer must have had an impact on me because my first degree was LLB Law.

We all had bicycles and I used to ride to church and everywhere with friends. I even used to meet friends at night, after school, riding around the streets, hanging out with young ladies. But we were only young and the worst we got up to was playing music and doing things those children that age would normally do.

I was an ordinary boy, with ordinary friends who liked riding our bikes, either on our own or in groups. I used to ride about half a mile on my own in the dark to get home and I wasn't afraid anymore, unlike when I was younger.

Now I was a bit older, a bit more mature, wiser and braver I would ride home feeling good about myself, of course always looking out for any crocodiles or police who might want to stop us for riding our bicycles sometimes without lights when the road was extremely dark. I guess you just get used to the roads where you were born and grew up. I loved the area and knew it like the back of my hand. I felt blessed to be born in that community and that environment because it laid a good foundation for my life.

At the same time, I was trying to get myself a girlfriend; everyone wants someone to love and be loved by them. Sometimes we would go to parties and hang out with our friends, standing to one side, watching others dancing, not dancing ourselves. Unlike my friends, I didn't drink alcohol, just something cool and nice but we were still hanging out at the wrong place at the wrong time. God was good to us.

By now, my mum was living in Kingston with my younger brother Roxroy and my cousin Kevin. I enjoyed going there in the long summer holidays. I played football with the guys, hung out with them on the streets in the volatile part of Kingston where my mum lived. On one occasion we had to run from the soldiers who used to drive across the train line from time to time. They would beat us up if we were caught on the street. We always had to run and hide from the police and soldiers. We didn't often stay out on the streets after 11 pm where we lived in Seaview Gardens, right beside the train lines.

One day we were sitting outside our yard and suddenly saw the soldiers coming in their Jeep. One of the guys said to us "Babylon is coming" and when we heard that we knew we had to scatter. We ran down the little alleyways behind the house, escaping from the soldiers, even though we weren't doing anything wrong. You didn't have to do anything wrong to get beaten up by them. I was so scared I ran into the house and hid in a bedroom. I was worried in case they'd seen us disappearing and would come in the house, drag me out and beat me up and maybe call the police to arrest me.

The way we generally travelled to Kingston was with other folks from my community, in a big lorry, which went there every Sunday, not only carrying people but straw to be sold in Kingston. The straw would be packed in the lorry all the way to the top. Space was made for older people to sit low inside the back of the lorry, but whenever I got a lift on it, those of us who were younger had to climb up on top.

Once, one of the kind ladies gave me a sheet to cover me on top of the cold lorry. Sometimes we would be driving all night and it was cold and windy in the open back, not to mention dangerous. When we arrived safely at the Coronation market, my mum would either meet me there or I'd get a bus down to Seaview Gardens. I had my little bag and whatever goodies I had brought from the country to give to my mum. Approximately 5 years ago there was an accident with that lorry and a young lady sadly passed away. I made that perilous journey so many times back in the late 80s and early 90s, I give God praise for His goodness in keeping me safe.

Kevin learned to make proper kites while he was living in Kingston, which we would fly in the yard. One night I dreamt that we were flying a kite in the yard and it escaped out of our hands and flew over the Jamaica Public Service unwrapped electric wire on the road and this separated the cord from the kite with a spark of fire. The level of anxiety was high when I told Kevin that we had to fly our kite over Mr Evans's land, not in the yard which was too near to the road and electric wire. The flying was in full swing; what could go wrong because we were so far away? Without a moment's notice, the kite was out of my hand, instantly we started chasing it. However, the wind was too much for us and it landed on the wire beside the guinep tree. Instantly the spark was unmistakable. I tried my best to avert the dream, however, the dream could not be stopped and it had to be fulfilled.

One day, when I was about 14 or 15 years old, I decided, as usual, to go to Great Pond. It was a lovely day and it had been raining a lot so we knew it would be a good time to do some net fishing, so off we went to Great Pond at the edge of Tar Yard. We put the net across the pond to catch most of the fish going across in the night. When we came back to retrieve our net in the morning, I eagerly went to the water mouth where my granddad's boat was moored and met up with my fishing partner. We took the boat out and headed for the net, wondering if we had a good catch.

We went to one end of the net, lifted it up and put it in the boat. Each time we put parts of the net in the boat, we'd take out all the sticks and other debris and put the fish into the boat. That day we had the best catch ever, the net was so heavy with fish I was very excited as I paddled my boat quickly to the net.

There were so many fish, some weighing between 10 and 20 pounds, some massive fish we called Tarpon. It was such fun taking out the fish and those Tara Pan. They were a silver colour but could look white under the water.

I saw this massive fish or at least what appeared to be, as I pulled the net closer to me. I thought it was a massive Tarpon, must have weighed over 100 pounds. I pulled the net up close to reach it with my hand and take it out of the net and into the boat. I was so shocked when I realised it was a crocodile, caught overnight in the net. It had drowned, probably while trying to eat as many fish as possible and somehow got entangled in it. That crocodile would be approximately 6 feet long and when I saw the teeth and the mouth, I was scared to death and dropped it straight back into the water.

I was now wondering how on earth I could get the rest of the fish out. I didn't have the courage at that age to take a crocodile out of the net and into a very small boat. I kept thinking how would we get the net back in the boat? How would we get home? The boat was just a small cotton tree boat, not one of those massive fibreglass ones.

Just then, I looked up and recognised Brother Ledgister from our church at the far end of the lake. He had a large, fibreglass boat and he was much more experienced than we were. I was so relieved to see him coming up towards us. I told him our plight that we had a crocodile in our net and we didn't know how to get it out. We needed to get the rest of our fish. We were so relieved when he assured us, he would help.

He took the net up gently and looked at the crocodile, then touched it with his paddle. We all watched with bated breath, to see if the crocodile was either going to spring on him or if it really was dead because none of us knew how long it had been caught in the net. When he was convinced that it had died, he took the net up and put the crocodile in his own boat.

He finally came in with a crocodile facing out from the front of his boat and we took it to its final resting place. It was a sad day indeed, a day of bittersweet, mixed feelings, and feelings of happiness because of the good catch that we had but sadness that the crocodile had died in the net because normally we work together in the water with crocodiles. We don't trouble the crocodiles and they don't trouble us. Crocodiles had never eaten anyone in that lake as far as we knew, even though its crocodile-infested water they do their thing in the water and we do our thing. We have a common goal, we are all trying to catch fish, and the crocodile is trying to catch fish to eat while we are trying to catch fish to eat and to sell. That crocodile was the same height as me. Generally, people were baptised in this crocodile-infested water.

5

A Pause on The Journey and a Time of Great Sorrow

July 1991 brought a bittersweet experience. I felt that for the past five years, I had done my best and worked hard to send myself to school. Now it was time for graduation and I had to move on. I'd made many friends, two from high school, in particular, Albert and Howard; we went everywhere together, in fact, we still communicate to this day. Preparing for graduation brought its own problems. I needed a grey suit, a white tuxedo shirt, bowtie, black shoes and a gown ("regalia") was hired. Everything else had to be purchased out of my personal income since I was working and studying. Every evening in the months before graduation, we practised the march to make sure we got it right. A male and a female, the head boy and the head girl at the front and the rest of us would follow in alphabetical order. The young lady I marched with was really nice, a pleasant young lady, a beautiful young lady, the type of girl every boy would like to march with. I felt privileged to have her as my marching partner; Admittedly, I was also a handsome young man.

I went around Black River buying all these things on my own. My mum, who took me to the school the first time I went there, supported me throughout my school life with her limited resources. She would have been happy to support me in finding all that I needed for my graduation. Nonetheless, things had changed dramatically and my mum who had been so healthy and strong five years earlier was now really unwell at just 39 years old.

Knowing that she was so sick, my mum asked my auntie Cherry to support me on the day of the graduation.

"I would love to go but I can't make it," she told me sadly.

My aunt and her daughter Judy came. On July 7th 1991, Marlene and Albert from my community were graduating as well, so we asked the taxi drivers to make a couple of trips for the people who had shown interest in attending along with us. I turned up for graduation really early and went to the library to get my regalia. I had a nice haircut from my barber. I found my regalia and nervously put it on, then lined up for the marching.

When the music started, we marched forward onto the school lawn. Our song at the graduation was "God is watching us from a distance" which we all sang and I found it really beautiful. I walked up for my certificate and received it with pride, by the grace of God. After graduation, it was a really hard time because we went around greeting friends, some of whom we knew we would never see again unless we happened to bump into each other in later life. We talked and laughed and when I arrived back home quite late that Sunday night, I felt a sense of pride, a sense of accomplishment. Yes! We have done it, not by might, or by power but by my spirit said the Lord (Zachariah 4: 6).

I felt that my mother's hard work, dedication, and commitment to have her children study at the secondary level had paid off. A year after her death, my younger brother went to secondary school as well. It certainly was not in vain. She wasn't there to see me graduate but at least she knew about my graduation. She saw me dressed for the graduation; she watched me iron my clothes and by then I could iron for myself, which she taught me to do. God kept my mum alive for those two days to see me finish. She died two days after my graduation. The Lord wanted her to see my graduation; she took me to both infant and secondary schools, so it was great that she witnessed my graduation and saw my certificate.

We would never see some of those whom we graduated with again in this life. Just two months after that ceremony in July, the beautiful, young lady whom I marched with sadly passed away at the tender age of 17. I was living in Montego Bay at the time of her passing so I did not have the privilege of going to her funeral.

The following day my mum was unwell. After coming back from fishing, I fried some dumplings and fish and my mum had a little for her breakfast but she struggled to eat.

I was out and about fixing the brake on my bicycle and a few other things that needed attention. I had been riding bikes for so long, I knew how to strip it down and spray it and put it back together again. I spent all that Monday working on it.

Early Tuesday morning, July 9th my mum asked me to go and call Brother Forbes. I told him that my mum was very sick and please could he take her to the doctor straight away? He leapt out of his bed and soon got her to the doctor beside Waterloo Guest House, not far from the courthouse in Black River. Plums were in season; two plum trees were in the yard of the doctor's office. Brother Forbes, my mum and I sat there waiting for the doctor for about 2 hours before he opened. While we waited, I was picking the plums to give to my mum for breakfast.

That time of waiting provided some of the best and most intimate moments I had ever spent with my mum. We talked about old times and about the church.

"When I am better," she said to Brother Forbes and me. "I will be going to church every single week. I have recommitted my life fully to God, no one will stop me from getting my Crown, no one will stop me seeing the face of my Jesus."

I went in with her to see the doctor and after examining her, he told my mum they had given her the wrong medication. Whatever they had said was wrong with her wasn't the problem at all. He then gave her a new set of medication, which she should take immediately. He gave us the prescriptions and on our way home, I stopped by my cousin Sandra's office and asked her if she could please help to get the prescription for my mum, which she did, willingly. I purchased some food, the medication, Complan Food Supplement and a bicycle brake cable. I also bought Patty and Coco bread, which was always a favourite.

When we arrived home, I was told that granddad wanted us to get firewood to cook on.

"You can let the others go," my mum said to me. "But you need to stay with me in case I need you."

"I will be just under the mango tree at the front of the house, fitting my brake cable, Mama Yet," I said. "If you need me, just call and I will be right there."

Later, she called to me urgently and I came running.

"Otis," she said. "I am really hot and I am unable to breathe, please fan me."

I was using a book cover to fan her, sitting beside her on the bed, hugging her and reading the Lord is the Shepherd I shall not want in Bible Psalm 23 to her, which she requested. It was painful, difficult and hard to watch my mother struggling for breath. Clearly, she could not breathe; it was as if the only breath she was getting in her body was from the fan.

"I am going to die, Otis. I'm going to die. I'm going to die," she cried.

"No, Mama Yet," I said. "You're not going to die."

I remember hugging her and praying with her and praying for her, fanning her and sweating with her. As a young Christian, I had been baptized three years earlier; I had faith in God. I knew that God would save my mum.

"Mama Yet," I kept repeating. "You're not going to die. Do you want me to call Brother Forbes again because you're really not looking well?"

"Yes," she replied. "Go and call him but please don't leave me too long."

I rode as fast as I could. When Brother Forbes came, I called my uncle Ronnie, to let him know that my mum wasn't well. I asked if he could follow her to the hospital. I told my mum that I couldn't come with her to the hospital this time. Actually, it was all too much for me to bear. I did not like how she looked, I thought on what she said, I was going to die and I didn't want to see my mum die so I didn't follow her to the hospital, my uncle did. My mum sat in the van beside him, struggling to breathe. It was approximately 2 pm. As soon as they drove off, I went into the next room and watched the van leaving with my mum. That was the last time I saw her alive.

I was hoping, I thought that maybe she would stay a couple of days, or a couple of weeks in the hospital, even a couple of months and then come back home. She didn't have any major sickness like cancer, stroke or high blood pressure; personally, I thought she only had a bit of pneumonia. I felt so weak I could not stand. I took my aunt Dora's radio; my cousin Richard had some nice tapes with Jim Reeves and other singers. I was playing the music and lying on the bed crying my eyes out, asking God to save my mother's life. I'd never prayed like that before. I'd never been in that type of trouble before but now I prayed earnestly, sincerely I wanted my mother restored to full health. She was still young, only 39 years old.

That night, my cousin Richard and my uncle Roland said they were going to take some food into the hospital for my mum. I watched them rode away. That night, my mum did not come back home after being admitted to Black River Hospital, they realized that she was so unwell. I went to bed very weak within my spirit, very worried. My dad was alive but he wasn't around and I wished he was because at least I could talk to him, at any rate, he could comfort me. I was 17 years old and I needed the comfort of a father figure at that time more than ever before.

I was in bed at about 9 o'clock that night, July 9th 1991, when I heard my cousin's bike roll up and we all got up to find out if he had any news of my mum and what was the latest from the hospital? We did not need to ask him because my uncle Roland was crying so hard. Then they said Mama Yet was dead! My world shattered, I felt so numb I could not move, I could not cry, I could not do anything, I just stood there transfixed wondering if I was in a dream and if so, could someone please wake me up. How could my mother die just two days after my graduation? She had done everything for me, she was my world, my rock; she was the one when I was down, I could speak to in the absence of a father. She had been both mother and father to me. How would I survive without my mum? Could I survive without her? She was everything to me. The world stood still, my world wasn't going anywhere and how could it go somewhere without the driving force in my life, my mum? From the very day I was born until that day, my mum had always been the driving force in my life. Without her, how could I carry on? My world has just lost its axis.

I remembered how, years earlier, I had told myself that if my mum should ever die before me, then, they should bury me with her. That's how much I loved my mum. When I look in the mirror, I see the image of my mother, I resemble her so much. I loved her and I would give the world for her. How could she have gone so soon at just 39 years old? My heart was broken and bleeding. Clearly, if in this life only we have hope we would be people most miserable (1 Corinthians 15: 19). Admittedly, the LORD will be a refuge for the oppressed, a refuge in times of trouble (Psalm 9: 9). Weeping may endure for a night, but joy cometh in the morning (Psalm 30: 5). "The LORD is nigh unto them that are of a broken heart; and saveth such as be of a contrite spirit", (Psalm 34: 18). "Blessed are they that mourn: for they shall be comforted" (Matthew 5: 4). "And God shall wipe away all tears from their eyes; and there shall be no more death, neither sorrow, nor crying, neither shall there be any more pain: for the former things are passed away" (Revelation 21: 4 KJV).

Finally, it hit me that she was gone and I would not see my mother again. The last time was when I was on the bed with her, hugging her and fanning her and telling her that she wasn't going to die. Finally, it dawned on me that was my last opportunity to be with my mum and I shall cherish those memories as long as God gives me breath, those precious moments with my mum will never be forgotten.

That was the worst night of my life. I lay there wide-awake, twisting and turning until the light appeared at the window. I wondered what would happen today, my first full day without my mother. I had a keen need for my father to be around because if one of my parents were there it would cushion the effect of the pain and distress, caused by the passing of my dear, precious Mum.

As I stumbled out of bed that morning, my head felt very light. My world had shattered and life didn't make sense. Then I remembered what Jesus said in the Bible that when your mother and your father are not there anymore, I will take you up (Psalm 27: 10). I heard the promises of God echoed by David, I have been young and now I am old and I have never seen the righteous forsaken nor the seed begging bread (Psalm 37: 25). I knew for a fact then that God would take care of me, that God would see us through as a family. I held onto the promises of God because I'm sure that God would find a way when there seemed to be none.

As bad as the pain was for me, I thought of how my younger brother must be feeling. He was only 11 years old and had lost his father approximately three years previously. Now he had lost his mother, how would he cope? Our dad was still alive but he lived far away and wasn't involved in our lives at all. Nevertheless, he was alive and while there is life, there is hope. However, I felt it more for my little brother and I prayed for him more than me. At least I was 17, just graduated from high school and my mum saw me graduating from Black River High School, but he had not even started high school yet. What would happen to him? I thought of my older brother as well. He was in Montego Bay and couldn't be here with us for the last moments. How would it affect him? My other family members, my aunt and uncle abroad, my grandparents, she was the first child out of 10 who had died and my grandparents by now were in their early 70s, how would they cope?

As the day rolled on, plans were being made for her funeral service, where and when she would be buried, who would be coming from abroad, what time of day the funeral would take place, all these things and at the same time, we had to make plans for the wake night (setup), getting food for people who were coming in to give us their regards, to pray with us, to send us their condolences and let us know that we were in their prayers. At the same time, we had to be thinking about food and drink for them, making plans and cooking. This situation was hard, it was tough but God gave us the strength (Philippians 4: 13 & 19).

At the same time, I remember some songs that we were playing, loudly for all to hear. "Oh, if I miss heaven, it would be better if I weren't born, for what would I say to God when I meet him on the judgment throne? I would be so confused if I am refused to enter the Promised Land," by Glen Graham. Then the grave-digging men came to help us to dig the grave, right there in the yard, under the big greengage mango tree. My heart sank. I asked myself each day, was this for real? I was hoping that someone would wake me up from this horrible nightmare that I was having and say to me it's not real. Unfortunately, there was no-one to wake me and the person who needed to be awakened was my mum who was now sleeping in Jesus (1 Thessalonians 4:13- 18; Revelation 14: 13 Matthew 27: 52), and the only one who could bring her back from the dead would be the life-giver, Jesus Christ Himself (John 1: 1- 4; John 5: 28, 29; John 11: 25; John 14: 6).

I know one-day Jesus will say: "gather my saints together

unto me, those who have made a covenant with me by sacrifice" (Psalm 50: 5). I know one day Jesus will wipe away all tears from our eyes (Revelation 21: 4), because even in writing this about my dear mother, my heart is aching, as if someone has placed a knife through it. After nearly 30 years, I'm not trying to get over my mother's death, I will never get over it. I'm just trying to understand and as much as possible to live with the reality of her not being here and try my best of course, in whatever circumstances I find myself to be content, because godliness with contentment is great gain (1 Timothy 6: 6). Admittedly, God has been good to me and has been good to all of us. The grave-digging starting in earnest and those who were digging the grave, calling for their white rum saying they needed to feed the other dead folks who were there and give them some white rum for protection. I remember them sprinkling white rum around the grave, while cooking was going on at the same time to give the gravediggers some solid food to eat. Admittedly, the Bible says, "For the living know that they shall die: but the dead know not anything, neither have they any more a reward; for the memory of them is forgotten" (Ecclesiastes 9:5). Evidently, no dead person was there because the dead person will only get life when Jesus returns (1 Thessalonians 4:16- 18 & John 5: 28, 29). I remember my church brother doing the sepulchre and as he made the grave and had everything ready, we were going back and forth ready for 28th July, the following Sunday when we would lay my dear mother to rest.

I remember all three Sabbaths between my mum's passing and her funeral day on the 28th of July 1991. I was present in the church; it was a hard medicine but I did not give up on God. To whom would I go if I had given up on God? He was my source of life, my salvation; He's the one who would keep me in this challenging time. I could not give up on Him hence my faith was still bright. I remember family members saying to me why do you have to go to church every week, now your mum has died, don't you think you can stay home? If I had stayed home, I know I would get caught up in doing a lot of things that should not be done on the Sabbath. I told them I'm going to do all that I need to do before the Sabbath but when Saturday comes around, that's God's day I'm going to be in the church, serving the Lord. That's what I did; to the glory of God, I was in church every single week I did not skip a beat.

When the time finally came, that infamous Sunday of my mother's burial, it was difficult. As I got dressed, I kept thinking of how, just three weeks earlier I had been searching for clothes to wear for a special occasion, my graduation. Now I was searching for clothes to wear at my mother's funeral; it was tough. As all of us got dressed, we were crying and sobbing. It was mournful but finally, we all got ready.

Some of us went in my uncle Clenert's car to Hilltop Seventh-day Adventist Church, the same church that I was a member of as was my mother before me. My auntie Lucy also had a car and took people up to the church, where the funeral service was held for my loving mum.

As we were driving in uncle Clenert's car, we passed a neighbour's house that was having a dance party. I wondered how could someone be having a party at a time like this when our hearts were broken? How could our neighbours be having a party? I thought that life should stand still at the passing of my mum because that's what happened to my own world, it stood still.

Then I remembered that when other people had lost their loved ones in the community, we continued with life as normal and it dawned on me that one person's passing will not stop the world rotating around the sun and life continues no matter how many people passed away. We will continue until Christ comes again. Hence, Christ asked when I return would there be faith in the earth? Will there be people on earth? Will the earth be populated or will the earth collapse in one final destruction called World War Three and the answer, the Bible gives is yes, there will be people on earth when Christ comes again, they will be there to see Him and some will be running to the rocks and the mountains and say fall off and hide us from the face of Him that sit upon the throne (Luke 18: 8; Matthew 25: 31, 32; Revelation 1: 7 & Revelation 6:15-17).

As we drove in the rental car, my world was torn apart when I got to the church and saw the hearse already there with loud music, knowing that the person inside it was my mum. This song springs to mind, "undertaker please drive slow because the lady you are taking is my mum and I hate to see her go." I went into the church and when they brought my mum and laid her in the church, it was tough. I went up to see if the person inside the casket was really my mother. I touched her and I called her name. I screamed and cried and called Mama Yet come back to us, don't leave us. When I grabbed her, she felt cold, she was stiff she could not respond to me. As I write this, I have to stop and weep because it seemed so real, like it was just yesterday and everything is still so raw, so fresh and as I remind myself of what took place nearly 30 years ago, I can hardly stop myself from crying.

I remember holding my mum, shaking her, calling to her telling her please come back to us we love her. It broke my heart to see my mum like that, unable to move, unable to respond to us. Then it dawned on me that she was gone, she had died. She passed away two weeks ago and now there was no more life in her, she was cold. If I had the power, I would have resurrected her. I prayed for her and I wasn't afraid to cry in front of everyone. I asked God to bring her back but nothing worked, my mum at 39 years of age, a young lady in her prime, who would have been 40 in September, she had gone too soon. She could not go back to her home again neither would we see her again until the Second Coming of Jesus Christ (Job 7: 8-10; 1 Thessalonians 4: 16-18; 1 Corinthians 15: 51- 58).

I said she's gone, but she will never be forgotten. I know Mama Yet lives on within my heart and that as long as I'm alive, I will cherish the memories. I'll do my best to continue her legacy. She did her best for us. We tried our best but nothing would help; we could not bring her back to life, no matter how we screamed and called my mum, her spirit had gone back to God who gave it to her in the first place. Her body going back to the dust whence it came (Ecclesiastes12: 7). I tried to hold onto her but I had to let her go.

She was so young, I never dreamed of losing my mum so early, before I was even 18. About four weeks before school graduation, I remember one of my schoolmates lost his mum and I thought then I don't know how I would be able to survive without my mum. Then seven weeks later I was burying my own mum.

I remember letting her go and I had to sit at the front of the church, in the section for family. I sat there through the first reading, the second reading, all the different items on the program, the eulogy, the sermon and believe me, nothing could console me. As I looked at my family members, they were all crying so were the members of the church. My mum had been a very peaceful lady in the community. She never troubled anyone. I never heard her argue with anyone. She was loving, peaceful, kind, caring someone with a heart of gold. I know everyone says this of his or her mum but believe me, I'm not the only one who said this of her. Everyone in the community said how Miss Lizeth was a very decent, polite lady. I never even heard her arguing back with her parents and she lived with them for 39 years generally, not one bad word from her.

There's a saying that God always takes the best. And indeed, that is so true because the word of God declares that God so loved the world that he gave his best, His only-begotten Son that whosoever believes in Him should not perish but should have eternal life through Jesus Christ our Lord and Saviour (John 3: 16).

After the service, we made our way outside. I'm not sure how I managed to walk but I got into the car, which took me home. Even though it was a bright sunny day, it was raining in my heart. This was the storm of my life, worse than hurricane Gilbert that I experienced three years earlier. It was sunny but a day of a hurricane, of a storm, a day of thunder and lightning. Unlike Gilbert, this hurricane would continue for the rest of my life. From time to time I would be in the eye of the storm but at other times I would be right in its heart. This storm will rage for the rest of my life but it's a storm that I know will not rage forever, even though it is relentless in its fury. The day is coming when the one who stood in the ship with Peter and the disciples and said peace be still (Mark 4: 39), is the same one who is able to bring peace to my troubled heart and all the troubled hearts around the world today and that one is the life-giver, Jesus Christ (Isaiah 40: 1 & 2).

On my way home, everything was blurring, nothing was clear. I was one of the first to take up my position beside the grave, as the undertakers and the pallbearers took my mum in. When I saw them lay her in the grave and the preacher about to do his last rites over my beloved mother, I was crying uncontrollably. No one could stop me from crying. My cousin Karen, I will never forget her, we were the same age just graduated and she held me in her arms and comforted me at the time when I needed comfort the most.

In the end, my mum was finally buried and then plans were being made for different things and to move on but how could I move on? What would I be moving on to, without my beloved mother? That night was tough because reality finally hit home, that my mum was now laid in the grave, cold and silent, concrete poured on top of the grave, no way of her breaking through that. Everything was cold and silent. Nevertheless, the hymn says "The mossy old graves where the pilgrims sleep shall open as wide as before, And the millions that sleep in the mighty deep shall live on this earth once more." The Bible says, "Marvel not at this: for the hour is coming, in the which all that are in the graves shall hear his voice. And shall come forth; they that have done good, unto the resurrection of life; and they that have done evil, unto the resurrection of damnation" (John 5: 28 & 29). "Jesus said unto her, I am the resurrection, and the life: he that believeth in me, though he were dead, yet shall he live" (John 11: 25). My mum had died and for her, the incredible dream was now a nightmare, the journey had ended, whereas mine had just begun. I just graduated and I had my entire life ahead of me. Sometime during that week, it could have been Tuesday or Wednesday, after laying my mum to rest on Sunday, my uncle came to me.

"Otis," he said. "You need to go to Montego Bay to stay with your brother Albeno. Cool off, clear your head, take it easy and then come back and see what you want to do."

He also assured me that I could go back to school, to the sixth form. He asked if I could find out how to go about it, he would finance it for me because my mother was now dead and there was no father in the picture to give moral, financial or spiritual support, so he would take up the responsibility, unfortunately, this did not materialize. He would send me to school to further my education and he said he was proud of me that I graduated from Black River High School. I took his advice and I went with him to Montego Bay.

6

Montego Bay

I decided to take my uncle's advice to go to Montego Bay. He drove me to where my brother lived in Mount Salem. I was so excited because it was only the second time I had ever been there. I had spent much more time in Kingston in the past. Once I got to Montego Bay, I enjoyed looking at the Hip Strip, with the beautiful hotels and beaches and so many people walking about; it was all so different from Saint Elizabeth.

I thought maybe there could be a future for me in Montego Bay, after the passing of my mum. I was only 17 years old. My brother who was 18 took me into the house where he was sharing a room with one of his friends who also asked his own cousin to stay from time to time when the guy was unable to go to the countryside where his family lived. So, I found myself in Montego Bay with three young men sharing one room and sleeping on the same bed. Thankfully, two of us, my brother who was a security guard and another roommate, worked at nights. Consequently, two of us would be there in the night-time generally and we later became best friends. It was quite tricky living there. The financial situation was really tough, even though we liked the lifestyle.

I went to the clubs with them, exploring the different nightlife, searching for what we never had. To be honest, we were each looking for a girlfriend or possibly, a wife but in all the wrong places. I met women from time to time and sometimes started a short relationship, hoping to fill the void left by my mother's passing. Then the finances weren't able to keep up; I have never felt hunger in my life like that before. God bless my late auntie Dora who would give me money regularly to help out. She was a lifesaver, really kind and loving auntie, I will never forget all that she has done for me.

I stayed in Montego Bay from the end of July until October 1991. I looked back on the life I had in Saint Elizabeth and felt like the Prodigal Son (Luke 15: 11- 32.) At least if I returned there, I would be sure of dinner from my granddad every night, even if it was some good gungo peas or beef soup I wouldn't starve. Anyway, whenever I was hungry in Saint Elizabeth, I could go to the mango tree. There were so many fruits to pick, unlike Montego Bay where you had to buy everything.

It came to the point where I had no money and I was so hungry I felt as if I was starving. Sometimes for days, it would be one meal and not one solid meal either. Things were really tough then. I quickly lost a lot of weight and like the Prodigal Son, I said to myself I will arise and go back to my grandfather's house, so that's what I did. In October, I packed all my stuff, got my fare and went back home to Saint Elizabeth to live, just months after moving away to Montego Bay for a new life.

I did try to get several jobs there but I was mainly turned down because I refused to work on the Sabbath day and I was told that I needed more experience. I told them I was willing to work from Sunday until Friday evening but on Saturday which is the Sabbath, I couldn't work because it's not my day, it's the Sabbath of the Lord thy God (Exodus 20: 8 - 11; Ezekiel 20:12 & 20; Mark 2: 27 & 28; Revelation 1:10). I successfully landed a few jobs, mainly in clothes stores, but they said Saturday was their busiest day and they needed me to be at work then. They offered to give me one or two Saturdays off but the rest of them

I had to be at work on a Saturday. I sadly shook my head and told them I couldn't do it. I had no money, no help or support, but I was determined to keep the Sabbath of the Lord holy and sacred at 17 years old.

I was offered a job in Sinclair's Bargain Centre but because of the Sabbath, I had to turn it down. Ethan and I used to walk along the Hip Strip, trying to find a job in this tourist hot spot in Montego Bay even maybe we could find a lady from abroad who could be our ticket to a new life where she lived but all the hotels turned us down, saying we were too young and didn't have any experience. I kept wondering how I could get experience in the hotel industry at 17 if they didn't even give me a chance to work in a hotel.

Years later, God has blessed me so much that I have now actually stayed in many of those hotels on trips back to Jamaica. Things that they believed I wasn't good enough for, I was now able to pay for and to pay people to do service for me. If God is with you who can be against you? If God is for us why should we fear (Romans 8: 31)?

At one point, we decided that we would even take work, washing dishes and pots in the kitchen. I certainly had experience in washing pots and plates at home. I was very handy and able to do everything before my mum died so surely that wouldn't be a problem. My mum taught me to wash my clothes when I was 9 years old. By the time I was 12, I washed all my school clothes and my church clothes. So, washing, ironing, cooking and cleaning presented no problem to me at all. I remember crying sometimes when my cousins used to tease me and say my mum didn't love me because she taught me to wash and cook and clean from so early on. But after she passed away, I realized why she had done that. By 17, I could do everything for myself. I was even able to iron all my clothes to perfection.

I went to a particular hotel, asking for work in the kitchen, washing pots. The pots turned out to be over 3 feet tall and still I was told I hadn't got enough experience washing pots, so they couldn't accept me. I finally reached my wit's end, still determined to remain a Christian and to serve God, in spite of the difficult circumstances.

When life got too much for me and I went back to Saint Elizabeth, I still had to find work there. I thought if there was no work for me in Montego Bay, what could I find in Saint Elizabeth, a much less developed Parish. At least Montego Bay was the second city of Jamaica and if I couldn't find work there, what could I do to make a living in the crocodile-infested, ghost town parish of Saint Elizabeth?

However, it should be noted that Saint Elizabeth is the breadbasket of the entire island of Jamaica. It was to Jamaica what Bethlehem was to Israel (Matthew 2; Luke 2). I had learned carpentry and cabinetmaking at school and I decided I would do that for a while. I went to a local cabinetmaker in the community and he was kind enough to offer me a job. He said I could come and learn the trade and he would give me something each week according to the work I did. When I started my new job there, I was very thin but as soon as I became financially stable again, I ate well, knowing that there was no rent to pay, no bills for water gas or electricity, because my grandparents paid for everything, thank God for my grandparents.

I started very small by just sanding and cutting board and helping out. Very soon I was making such furniture as beds, chairs and tables, all within seven months because the following summer I would be going back to Montego Bay. I had been promised a job in a barber's shop there. The owner told me that when I was 18, he would employ me as a barber, a job I had never done in my life. How on earth would I learn barbering in such a big and fast city as Montego Bay?

While I was working in Saint Elizabeth, I used to go out on my bicycle in the night-time with my friends. We were much older now and on the lookout for girls and to have a good time. We would do that at nights and on the Sabbath, I would be in the church. Even though I would not work on the Sabbath I wasn't a perfect person.

Although I wouldn't work on the Sabbath, even if I was starving, at 17 I wouldn't do that. It had been instilled in me at an early age. On the other hand, I would be out there looking for girls, chatting them up. I was going out trying to have fun. I was trying to find a life partner, someone that I could share the rest of my life with. There were a few people I started a relationship with but nothing really serious.

In the summer of the following year, I left Saint Elizabeth and went back to Montego Bay; my second time around trying to salvage what went wrong the first time. Again, I stayed with my brother and his two friends and at one point I stayed with my cousin Dawn one will always be grateful for these accommodations. I spoke to the owner of the barbershop and let him know that I was back and I'd like to start learning to cut hair with him. My friend Ethan had started barbering and told me how well he was doing, so I wanted to cut hair as well. Ethan promised to take me under his wing, even though he had only started himself four months earlier.

The owner decided to give me a chance so I started working

there. We did not exchange any words about the Sabbath, or my being a Seventh-day Adventist Christian, I was just learning. Sometimes I might just cut maybe one or two during the week. It didn't matter if I went to church on a Sabbath, I would be back at work from Sunday.

"Bro," I would say it to him when it came to Friday evening before sunset. "I'm going home now, see you on Sunday."

"No problem," he replied. "Take care of yourself."

The following week I did the same thing and left on Friday, telling him I'd see him on Sunday. Again, it was no problem. Then on Friday of my third week, he asked me to come in on Saturday because it was the busiest day. He'd noticed that I hadn't worked any Saturdays since I started. I didn't know what to say. I was determined by God's grace not to work on the Sabbath. I was sure that God would provide for me as the word of God declares that "my God shall supply all your needs according to his riches in glory in Christ Jesus" (Philippians 4:19).

"You know," I said. "I'm a Seventh-day Adventist Christian and unfortunately, I do not work on Saturdays. I really like the work down here and I'm willing to do my best from Sunday to Friday. However, then I have to go to church and I can't come to work on a Saturday. I've been a baptized member of the church for four years now and I've never worked on a Sabbath and unfortunately, I'm not prepared to do it now but I would really appreciate if you could keep me on. I'll do my best. I'll stay late and work early on six days a week but Friday evening I have to leave before sunset. I will even come back Saturday evening after sunset to work."

"You know what," he said to me. "One of my barbers is

leaving. He's going to his mother in America and I wanted to give you his chair. You could work that chair for yourself on a Saturday because he doesn't work on a Saturday and then when he leaves, you could get that chair for yourself and have your own Barber's chair."

"I'm so sorry," I said. "But I can't work on the Sabbath."

"Alright," he said suddenly. "I have to confess something. I am also a Seventh-day Adventist but unfortunately, because of the nature of my work, I have to work on the Sabbath. But I like how you stand up for your faith as a young man and what you believe in. I promised myself that I would never take another Seventh-day Adventist to work here because Saturday's my busiest day. But I'm gonna give you the chance because you've been working with me now for three weeks and your behaviour is impeccable. You're a very honest, respectful and dignified person and I want a person like you in my shop. So, even though you can't work on the Sabbath, I'm gonna keep you. Please come down after Sabbath and work."

From then on, I was able to learn the trade, which I did quite quickly. By my first Christmas, in less than 6 months I had caught up with the others who had been there for two years or more. God gave me skill and understanding and I mastered the trade by the grace of God (Daniel 1: 17). But then it's a dog eat dog world and you had to be tough sometimes and even give the appearance of being rough. I wasn't a rough person; I was a soft-spoken, quiet person. I was arguably the quietest person in the community of Little Bridge district, so how would I manage in a big city like Montego Bay?

My job required me to get out in the street and call people into our barber's shop. We'd all be out there shouting: "excuse me would you like a haircut?" If they said yes, you had to guide them into your chair, while the others were just waiting to take them off you before they could even get to your chair.

I did manage to master the art of getting people in my chair and I was so successful that some of the other guys were afraid of me. They were so happy when I wasn't at work because my eyes were always peeled, looking out for whoever was coming and because I knew I wouldn't be there on Saturdays, I needed to get as much work in during the week. I was always the first one there in the morning and the last to leave in the evening. I was just 18 years old at the time and I would open the shop for the owner and on most occasions, I'd close up for him as well. Wherever he sent me I was more than willing to go.

By the end of that year, I was earning more money than many married people with 3 or 4 children to feed. So, at the age of 18, I moved out of my brother's place and rented a home of my own. From that time on, I've been independent, paying my own bills and everything until this day.

While I was very serious and determined not to break the Sabbath, I would still be out on the streets with the guys and while we were waiting for customers, we'd be on the lookout for young ladies, calling out to them and giving them the sweet talk, telling them why we believed they should be ours. That was an art I picked up quite well too.

The following year, 1993, I had risen to the status of senior barber. Some older ones had left and newer ones were coming in, so I was now a senior. Whenever young ladies came into the shop or walked past, we'd be giving them the usual banter. One day, a young lady came in asking for her nephew's hair to be cut. As per usual I started chatting her up. It wasn't the time of mobile phones so you couldn't exchange numbers, or communicates on WhatsApp, Facebook or Instagram. Social media didn't come on stream for another 10 years, so no YouTube, or Twitter or anything like that. All you could do was make plans to meet up somewhere in Montego Bay.

This particular young lady became my girlfriend. She would come and look for me at the shop from time to time and we'd go out. I was still chasing other girls at the time, I had about two or three that I was talking to but she became the most regular one.

She used to come and look for me at the shop and I'd be there cutting hair. Then we'd go to the Dragon Gym and have a great time. All of us barbers would be well dressed and really enjoy ourselves, even though I was still a Christian. We knew how to dress. We would turn up for work in white shirts and black jeans at all times clean and sweet. I used to go to Falmouth on a Wednesday because they had a clothes market, selling all the latest fashions, including shoes.

I remember all of us guys going to the carnival on the Hip Strip of Montego Bay, trying to find a young lady from abroad who would be our ticket to a better life. We all wanted to go abroad like some of our friends had already done.

I was going far in the world, from one degree of worldliness to the next. If I'd continued down that road, it would have been a matter of when rather than if I would leave the church and leave my relationship with God, which was strained at the time. Moreover, I was determined to go with my mum wherever she was.

I had decided that whatever happened to my mum would happen to me. For example, I gave God an ultimatum, that if my mum had lost her way and does not make it to the Kingdom of Heaven, then I didn't want to go to heaven, I wanted to be with my mum and stay with her forever. And if she is saved, I will do my best by the grace of God's power and the Holy Spirit, to make sure I reach Heaven to be with her. I loved her so much; I just wanted to be with her wherever she was.

It was a complicated time in my life but honestly; I meant it when I said I was still hurting. I was broken, battered and bruised by the loss of my young mother, gone too soon. Never will she be forgotten; her children and her relatives remember the person that she was. My mum has left an indelible mark, which will stay with us all our lives.

God knows how to lead his children; He knows how to take care of us when we're down and depressed when we are discouraged and believe there's no way out. When we are about to leave Him because the enemy struck a deadly blow and challenged God. The enemy said, to the Lord, if you allow this horrible incident to happen to Otis, then he would curse you and turn his back on you (Job 1: 11 & Job 2: 5 & 6). God challenged the enemy and said; no he will still trust me. Admittedly, it was a close call; I got very close to the place where I was about to curse God and did as noted in the Bible. "Then said his wife unto him, Dost thou still retain thine integrity? Curse God, and die" (Job 2: 9 KJV).

I went to my bed one night and God showed me in a dream that my mum's Salvation was secure in Jesus Christ and that my mother had found a resting place in Jesus our Lord and Saviour, her life was hidden with God in Christ Jesus (Colossians 3:3). The Lord also showed me like the Apostle Paul that my mum could say "I have fought a good fight, I have kept the faith, henceforth, is laid up for me a crown of eternal life which the

Righteous Judge shall give me at that day and not to me only but unto all them also that love His appearing" (2 Timothy 4: 7 & 8).

This was indeed a supernatural encounter; I got up from my dream with renewed impetus, new zeal, new motivations and new strength, which propelled me forward. Only God could have given me this dream, no one else. I now knew that my mum found a resting place in Jesus. I will meet her again and then, that fearful Tuesday when I hugged her and cried with her and told her that she wasn't going to die, the last time I saw her alive. I will definitely see my mum again, where there will be no more parting, the circle will not be broken any more in heaven. Truly, then, I could say to my mum, you will never die again. That will be because we will be with God where we will reign with Him forever and eternally, we will be with the Lord (Revelation 21: 1- 7; John 11: 25, 26).

I was now determined to serve God because of the salvation that God showed me that my mum had found. Now I had confidence in God and I understood the word of God a little more. I felt certain that the enemy would not have given me such a dream, that my mother's soul was safe with God, so I would live for God. There was no way the enemy would tell me to live for God; I was convinced that this was God speaking to me in that dream. God was telling me to hold on and don't let the evil one deceive me.

7

Converted

That year, 1994, as senior Barber, things were going well, financially, emotionally and physically. I was teaching others how to cut hair. I had many customers and they all understood my availability. They all knew I didn't work on the Sabbath. I had a girlfriend and I was looking forward to continuing my life in this way. I sported the latest clothes, the latest shoes, my home was secure, I was living on my own and everything appeared to be going well by the grace of God. On top of this, I was managing to save money. Every week I went to the bank and deposited some money in my account. What more could I ask for? I had a girlfriend, a place to call my own and money put aside. I was young and healthy and things started to take a turn for the better. I was also beginning to deal with my mum's passing a bit better.

I heard about a campaign in Farm Heights, Montego Bay when I was living in the Glendevon area. Pastor Samuels was the preacher. I was determined to attend each night after work and I invited my best friend Ethan to go with me. I was always a lover of campaigns because it was spiritually uplifting, a good time to bring families together and of course; I also saw it as an opportunity to meet young ladies. Hence, I was determined to go there every night and certainly every Sabbath. I wouldn't miss that campaign for anything.

On the times that Ethan came with me, I noticed how he was touched by the power of the Holy Spirit. I had no idea the impact this would have on his life. He was a guy who was into a lot of girls at the time. He was also keen to work as much as possible and save money. He had many customers but if he gave up his Sabbath to come and serve God, he would have lost a lot of income. However, he was interested in the campaign and the more he kept coming, he decided to attend on the Sabbath as well.

I also invited my girlfriend to the campaign. I was hoping that she would give her life to God and kept inviting her again and again. I was moved by the power of the Holy Spirit as is typical in a campaign setting. I've always felt the Spirit of God whenever I have attended campaigns, so I knew it was a spiritually enriching time for me as a Seventh-day Adventist Christian as well, not just for my friends but I would benefit by being at this campaign.

One night, the preacher gave a powerful sermon, telling the story of his brother who had cancer and how he tried to encourage his brother to give his life to God. He made an appeal and I remember Ethan turning to me.

"Otis," he said. "I'm going down to the altar."

"I will go with you," I said.

And I went down to the altar when the appeal was made for those who would like to be baptized. My best friend was really moved by the power of the Holy Spirit and took a card to sign up for baptism. Honestly, I had mixed feelings about what would happen next. I thought, if he is a Christian, then a lot of the stuff we used to do together we wouldn't be doing anymore. So, we would miss many of the pleasures that we used to enjoy.

However, I also had feelings of great joy and happiness,

anticipating what was to come, now that my best friend would be walking the same road with me as a Seventh-day Adventist Christian. I knew we could do so much more together; I could teach him about God and the Bible, about the church and about what we believed in. We would stop doing some of the foolish things that we were doing and think more about our progress with God. We could think about ministry, about serving God. I would have someone at the shop with me who believed in the same thing and could stand together, firm as a rock against a time of temptation.

On Friday evenings, rather than me going home alone, we could go home together. We were living in the same flat and each of us had our own rooms, including the two other people who lived there in the four-bedroom house. We all shared a kitchen and a bathroom and we could play gospel music together. We loved listening to great gospel music on Love FM and also a range of cassette tapes that we could play. It would be sharing this with him.

At his baptism I was overwhelmed; I was over the moon that my friend was now a baptized member of the Seventh-day Adventist Church. We pledged to stop playing around and start serving the Lord wholeheartedly. I was determined to set a positive example for my friend who had just found Jesus. I was going to stop going out on the road with the guys, chatting up women; all of that would now be a thing of the past and I'd be a new person in Jesus Christ.

We returned to the barbershop to let them know that he was now a baptized member of the church and we were going to stop the hanky-panky. On Friday evenings we closed up together and set off home, stopping first at the Captain's bakery to get nice, fresh, hot bread, some peanut butter and ordinary butter. Then to the supermarket for some cereal, milk and snacks I needed for the Sabbath because I wasn't going to be cooking then.

In the morning I had cereal and bread and that would be my breakfast; no cooking on the Sabbath. We kept the Sabbath (Saturday) as stated in the Bible "Remember the Sabbath day to keep it holy" (Exodus 20: 8-11). The scripture says "Remember now thy Creator in the days of thy youth, while the evil days come not, nor the years draw nigh when thou shalt say, I have no pleasure in them" (Ecclesiastes 12: 1). Some other gems that helped me are "Wherewithal shall a young man cleanse his way? by taking heed thereto according to thy word. Thy word have I hid in mine heart, that I might not sin against thee" (Psalms 119:9,11). "Thy word is a lamp unto my feet and a light unto my path" (Psalms 119: 105).

Ethan had a customer who was a very serious Seventh-day Adventist Christian. He was a bit older than us and so happy to know that my friend was now a Christian and that I was taking Christianity seriously. He joined us and we all would link up from time to time. He came to see us at the shop one day and talked about the second coming of Christ. I was astonished to find a young man in his early 20s to be so brave and fearless in talking about God and the love of God. The entire shop was spellbound by the powerful words coming out of his mouth regarding the power of God in a future judgment.

The barbershop was changed forever when two very influential barbers made an about-turn. We no longer chose to play around on the street as we used to. There was new life, new vigour, new strength and the barbershop became a place where you not only came to get a haircut but to meet Jesus Christ because the Spirit of God was in that shop. That guy wasn't working at the time, so he could visit the shop each day and we would all talk about our newfound relationship with God and how much God had done for us. I was trying to get the others converted by the grace of God.

Our friend came to the barbershop every single day to talk about God. We would then go out and buy a healthy lunch. He told us that the world would be coming to an end, we had to be ready and what we needed to do, in order to be ready.

I remember clearly like it was yesterday, that morning I went to work very early, as usual, I went to the Express Restaurant on the same Plaza where I worked. I remember ordering brown stewed chicken with extra dumplings and took that food with me down to the shop, so I would not miss any customer and had my breakfast, either in the chair or outside. I really enjoyed that brown stewed chicken, especially with the extra dumplings.

Later that day when our friend came, we took a break and went down to Creek Street where there was a nice vegetarian shop, where we could get something healthy for lunch. We met Truly Truly there and we were talking about God and about the end of time. And I remember he said to us if anyone is eating meat when Jesus comes again, they would not be translated and go to heaven to be with Jesus because they're eating meat and the Spirit of Prophecy said you should not be eating meat because meat is not healthy for you. Clearly, the Bible teaches a healthy lifestyle generally, (Leviticus 11; Deuteronomy 14; 1 Corinthians 10: 31; 3 John 2) and specifically a vegan diet in Genesis 1: 29.

Remember I had just bought brown chicken stew with extra dumplings; would this prevent me from seeing the face of God? As far as I was concerned, we were taught not to eat unclean meat like pork for example but while we were eating clean meat, there was no problem. We just had to serve the Lord "in the beauty of holiness" (Psalm 96: 9). However, our friend was always telling us about being vegetarian. Our church Brother Truly Truly said anyone who is caught eating meat at that time will not be translated.

Both Ethan and I and were determined from that day on, never to eat meat again. We had no understanding at 19 years old what it is to be a vegan, living on our own with no parents to cook for us, and mainly living off food from restaurants. From breakfast to dinner we would be buying from restaurants. How would we survive as vegans? We went to the Montego Bay market and purchased a lot of fruit, oranges, apples, tangerines and bananas, and we decided to have that for our lunch. In the day we became vegan, at the start of the day I had my nice breakfast and by the end of the day, I was a full vegan so no meat, egg, cheese, no dairy product of any sort. Within a week I had lost so much weight it was unbelievable. I wasn't a big person to start with; I was always a slim person. I grew up slim not extra slim, but with a vegetarian diet, I became very slim. Clearly, this was not the recommended way to be a vegan; it was very dangerous but God kept me.

We learnt how to cook soya protein, vegetarian sausages and other vegetarian stuff such as tofu but we found them to be very expensive at that time. We would now have to learn a new way of cooking and a new way of eating. I stopped eating and drinking at the same time. I've never eaten without a drink before. I grew up having my tea and eating bread or eating something with my tea. If I was at school or in town, I'd have coco bread, patty and a drink at the same time. However, now we had to learn a new way of life and also not eat as often as we used to. We could not eat between meals so after eating we had to give our stomachs four or five hours to rest before we ate again.

I thought that if I could manage my appetite at this time then I would be able to manage everything else by God's grace. My friend and newfound brother in Christ and I would go home on a Friday evening and when we came back to the shop on Saturday night, they would tease us. I'd been putting up with that for over 2 years, so it wasn't a problem at all but to my friend it was really tough. They joked that his customers had come during the day and couldn't find him because he was at church, so they cut their hair for them and made so much money off his customers. Week after week they teased us and eventually, it got to my friend and newfound brother in Christ.

One Sabbath morning I was looking for him, to go to church together and I realized he was still in bed. I thought it was just a one-off thing because when I was getting ready for church, he said he would just have a lie-in today and wanted to stay home. When I realised he was back full-time at the barbershop, I resolved in my heart that even if I had to do it alone, I would continue to serve the Lord. I would never work on the Sabbath.

I continued going to church and this was the starting point of my conversion. I was now a converted young man. At 19 years old, I was determined to follow God, come what may I would not be shaken again by God's grace. I would not waver in my faith or go back to my old ways; my old lifestyle was now history.

From that day, they changed my name at the barbershop. They would not call me Otis anymore; from now on the other barbers called me Moses. I wasn't running around with them on the streets any more, I was standing like Moses stood at the burning bush and at the Red Sea (Exodus 3 & 14). I had met Jesus Christ and he called me to come closer to him Matthew 11: 28 - 30. He said take off your shoes from your feet for the ground on which you stand is holy ground and God said to me at that time I will send you to pharaoh and I said Lord I cannot even speak, I'm the quietest person in my house and the quietest person in my community. I cannot even speak Lord and God said to me who made your mouth, who created your mouth will speak through you (Exodus 4: 11). Use what you've got in your hand (Exodus 4: 2). And I accepted the challenge and was determined by the grace of God to use what I had in my hand, which was the Bible (Hebrews 4: 12).

From then on, when I went to work in the mornings, I would take my Bible with me. In the taxi, I would be reading my Bible. At that time, there were no iPads or smartphones to disguise your Bible and pretend you were reading a text message or something. I had the hardcover Bible so people could see a young man 19 years old, walking down the street with his Bible in his hand, every single day as if he was going to church. But I wasn't going to church, I was going to work and when I got to my chair, I would bow my head, close my eyes and I would pray right there in the shop. Even if customers were waiting for me, it didn't matter. I would sit in my chair and pray to God to bless me, to bless the day, to bless the customers and everyone in the shop.

The customers who used to admire me because I had a lot of my pictures on the mirror, displaying different styles where customers would like to be like me. They were now asking me what had changed in my life because I seemed like a totally different person. I told them that I was now converted and living up to my Christian faith. I would use that opportunity to tell them about the love of God in Christ Jesus. I would tell every person whose hair I cut, or who came into the shop about God (Isaiah 43: 10). I used that opportunity to witness to them about God and the love of God, to tell them how the Barbershop was our mission field, a mission field for God.

I would go to the Adventist Book Centre (ABC), every week to purchase small pamphlets and leaflets that I could give to each person who came in the shop and encourage them to read it. I would give them leaflets on the Sabbath, the Second Coming of Christ, the State of the Dead and other things as well. That was my mission. People would see me walking on the streets with my Bible and engage me in conversation, asking me if I was a Christian. I always took it as a great opportunity to tell them about the love of God which is in Christ Jesus our Lord (Romans 8: 38 & 39).

Even when I was riding in the taxi, people would see me with my Bible and ask me about God and the love of God and again I used it as an opportunity to tell everyone in the taxi about my saviour and my friend Jesus Christ (Acts 1: 8 & Matthew 28: 18-20).

Aged 19, I used to go out in the Glendevon community, Norwood and Green Pond, all of which was a rough area. We would go out, fearing no evil (Psalm 23: 4) and doing missionary work, telling people about God, about the love of God about what God has done for us and what God can do for them if they only accept Christ as Lord and Saviour. Many young people came to faith in the community. We never gave up; we kept telling people about God and the love of God.

By then, we used to have Sunday night evangelistic meetings

and invited people to come. Also Wednesday night prayer meeting and on Friday evenings, we had Bible studies and youth fellowship. On the Sabbath, we would have a powerful service, which we enjoyed it.

One Sabbath we went down to Freeport where we did fasting and prayer and on the Sabbath, we sang Faith of Fathers. Brother Brian was the preacher and he read from the Great Controversy, from the Spirit of Prophecy and Last Days' Events. We prepared how we would run in the time of trouble, with fasting all day. We were all young people and one older lady, on fire for Jesus Christ. When we went back home, we felt the power of the Lord moving in our lives that day. I will never forget when we were with God and nature in Montego Bay. The pretty blue Caribbean Sea was right beside us, splashing up on the beach while we were right there with God and it was powerful, to God be the glory.

Being a vegan took its toll on me and I got really slim. When I went back to visit my family members in Saint Elizabeth, they could not believe how I looked, I was so thin. They asked me if I had been unwell. I told them, no, but I'd changed my diet and was now a vegan. They begged me, beseeched me, they even threatened and did everything to encourage me to start at least eating chicken again.

My mum had just passed away two years ago now and clearly, they cared about me and did not want to lose me just two years after my mother's passing, so they did all in their power to help me to start eating meat again and at least drink milk, eat eggs and cheese, but to no avail. I am a very stubborn person and if I make up my mind to do something, I can be strong-willed. I was 19 and financing myself so I didn't need anyone to take care of me. I was not going to turn like the late Prime Minister

Margaret Thatcher said, "you turn if you want to but this lady is not for turning." So, this young man was not for turning either. There was nothing they could do to change my mind because I was convinced that I would be translated as a vegan and I love God so much, I would do anything to make sure that I was translated. I would work my way towards translation in this way. Evidently, this was wrong, no one can work his or her way to heaven. The Bible says for by grace you are saved not by works lest anyone should boast (Ephesians 2: 8 & 9).

In the meantime, my brain was clear as crystal. It was like God had given me a brand-new brain. I was studying my Bible daily. I was memorizing my Bible daily and within no time, I read my Bible from cover to cover, not merely reading but studying the word of God. I became transformed by the power of God; my spirit was renewed I was a new creature in Jesus Christ (2 Corinthians 5: 17). I know I learned in three months, what I did not know in five years of being in the church and being a Christian.

I would describe myself as a conservative at that time. I was quite traditional, even at just 19 years old; I was more conservative in my thinking about religion. I wanted to go back to my roots, the primitive religion and godliness. I was standing up for the right and I was living for the right and this time my Bible was my main food. It would be the first thing that I read in the morning and the last thing that I read before bed at night. In the daytime, if I wasn't cutting anyone's hair, I would take my Bible and I would sit there quietly reading it, eating up the word of God. Like in Revelation chapter 10 I heard a voice say son of man eat it up and I said give it to me and it was sweet in my mouth indeed the word of God is sweeter than honeycomb (Psalm 19: 10). The word of God was a lamp unto my feet and a light unto my path (Psalm119: 105). Where shall a young man cleanse his ways but by taking heed to the word of God (Paslm119: 9). Thy words have I hid in my heart that I may not sin against thee (Psalm 119: 11).

That was my daily bread and when I had a good knowledge of the Bible, I remembered that I had a book, which was given to me by that friend who used to come by the shop and talk to us about God. I started reading "The Spirit of Prophecy" by Ellen G. White. At first, I doubted a lady in the 20th century claiming to have the spirit of prophecy, the gift of prophecy. I said I want to know no other book but the Bible. However, I would give her a chance and read her, just to prove her wrong and prove those who believe that this lady is a prophetess were wrong.

I cannot remember at my baptism or any time, being told anything about Ellen G. White. Who was she anyway? So, I was not going to be quick to accept her as a prophetess. I would study her writings and prove her wrong. By that time, I had a very keen understanding and knowledge of the Bible. I had been to University but it was not the University of man, it was the university of the Holy Spirit. I had such a deep and profound understanding of the word of God, it was a knowledge way beyond my years (Psalms 119: 99). All of this came to me, not because of any good thing that I had done but as a gift from God, who has gifted me with the knowledge of His word (Matthew 5: 6; Jeremiah 29: 13; Proverbs 3:5, 6).

So, with a comprehensive knowledge of the Bible, I was in a good place to read and challenge Ellen G. White, the servant of God and prove Sola Scriptura the Bible and the Bible only. At least, that's what I thought. So, I set out on my journey through the "Spirit of Prophecy" to prove that there is no other prophet who would come or will come again, and it is for us now to accept the word of God as written in the Bible.

However, the more I read her, the more I came to understand that this lady was touched with the Spirit of God and indeed was blessed with the gift of prophecy. I read her even more and especially when I started reading the Great Controversy, was always pointing me back to the Bible. It was giving me all these texts from the Bible and with the keen knowledge I had of the Bible; I could go back to all of those texts, which I had memorised. By then you could just call maybe two words from scripture and I would tell you exactly the chapter and verse in the Bible where you can find it. People would say to me that I had such a good knowledge of the Bible and I'd say no, it's not me; it's a gift from God. They'd ask if I read the Bible a lot? I said I study my Bible every single day with a keen eye, to know God and to know Him more, not only to know God but also to conform my life according to the will of God. So, the more I learned from the Bible, the more I would apply my life and my heart unto the word of God. So, the word of God was not only something that I do but it became a part of my life. It was a way of life for me and I would live, eat, breathe, drink the word of God. I was so hungry at the time; I was so thirsty but then I could not have enough, I could not get enough of the word of God. The one who hungers and thirst for rigorousness shall be filled (Matthew 5:6; Proverbs 2: 4).

Being filled with the Spirit of God, I was determined by God's grace that I would continue to live for God. I invited my girlfriend at the time to the campaign, hoping that she would surrender her life to Christ and be a Seventh-day Adventist Christian, but she didn't. When she came to look for me as usual, I said to her that I have met Jesus Christ anew and I'm now converted. I wanted her to find this new relationship that I had found in Jesus Christ. We could continue together, make a life together, but I would like her to come to know Christ as Lord and Saviour first of all and then this relationship would be founded on Jesus Christ (Matthew 7: 24- 27).

I pleaded with her and preached to her but unfortunately, she was not ready to make the same commitment as I had, admittedly, she was still young. So, we came to a mutual understanding that this relationship would not go far in its current form. We would still see each other and indeed, we are still friends to this day. However, I was now thinking of getting married and surrendering the rest of my life to the work of God and the work of ministry ("The Incredible Dream").

"The Incredible Dream" was now calling me. I remember clearly, I went to my elder and said I would like to go to West Indies College, now the Northern Caribbean University, to study theology. I wanted to be a minister of religion. The elder said to me Brother Lewis, where you are in terms of your understanding of the Bible and the Spirit of Prophecy, you are so solid in the church I wouldn't recommend for you to go to West Indies College, because if you do you would have to unlearn everything that you have learned now and you would not be the same person when you came out. So, his encouragement for me as a young man who was so solid in the word of God was to become a lay preacher. He said we are free to preach the word, as you would like, with no one telling you what to preach or how to preach.

I took his advice on board and decided that I would be a lay preacher from now on. I did the lay preacher's course in 1994 to become an evangelist and a Bible worker; it appears that the "The Incredible Dream" had died. I quickly understood what they were saying because I was hungry, starving so I studied keenly and became a lay evangelist. I received a certificate as such and that's what I continue to use. The hunger and thirst, the urge to be a minister of religion did not go away, "The Incredible Dream" was still alive, at least, in my heart. As a lay preacher, I had to be working and doing my own thing but the urge was still there, the calling was still there to be a minister and it just would not go away. It was a fire that I could not quench, this thirst in my soul to be a full-time minister of the gospel, God had laid it on my heart and it would not come off until I finally fulfilled the will of God in my life.

The drive for full-time ministry was so strong; a thousand buckets of water could not quench it. So, I left the barbershop and all my colleagues and signed up to the colporteur ministry, or literature evangelist ministry in 1994. I continued this for about two months and realized that the finances weren't coming in and it wasn't what I had been expecting. I worked hard, travelling on the bus from Montego Bay to Westmoreland, walking everywhere with my briefcase. I travelled to Trelawney and searched every nook and cranny; introducing people to good, solid Christian books but the colporteur profession did not take off at all.

I would travel very far but unfortunately, no one was there, no literature evangelist was willing to take me under their wing and show me the ropes. It was a tough race, you had to learn on the job and with no one to help you, it was each person for themselves, at least that's how I found it. After walking all over Montego Bay, Trelawney and Westmoreland, trying to make ends meet, trying to sell good, valid Christian books with the hope of making thousands of dollars in return to keep myself going. Alas, I sadly and quietly had to give it up but it wasn't a sudden ending, it was hard for me to let go. I would go out in the mornings and then go to the barbershop in the afternoon and ask my Seventh-day Adventist colleague, Taddy, if he had an empty chair? He said yes, so I said OK I'll come and work in the evening, after finishing the other job. I went out as a literature evangelist in the mornings then went to work cutting hair.

In the end, I found myself not going out in the mornings at all, because nothing much was going on if the truth be told. So, like Peter I went back to fishing, I went back to what I knew and what I loved, barbering (John 21: 1-3). I continued doing barbering. Most of my customers had gone but I still found a few who knew I was already a senior at the shop before I left, so it wasn't that I was starting from scratch. In no time at all, I built up my clientele and started earning good money again. This was the money that I used to start my property in Saint Elizabeth. During the time after I left, I finally lost touch with my then-fiancée. There were no mobiles such as we have today and our relationship had already come to a natural end anyway, but with me away, it brought the situation to a head.

By 1994, as a young man of 20 years old, I went back to Saint Elizabeth to Little Bridge District and spoke to my granddad. I told him that I would like to build a house there and come back to live in Saint Elizabeth when it's finished. I asked him if he would be so kind as to permit me to build this house on his land? My granddad was also a Seventh-day Adventist Christian and he could see that I was now a different person, so he said, son, no problem at all.

He took me to a corner of the one-acre land that we grew up on and showed me the spot where I could build my house, right next to the fence. I thanked him so much and told him how much it meant to me to be able to start building my own house. At the age of 21, I started my first project of building my first home, with no help from mother because she had died four years ago and none from my father who was now living in New York. I had no financial help from anyone but great help from my granddad, he gave me the land.

However, of course, I had the richest person helping me so, to be honest, I should not really say I didn't have any help because God indeed helped to build my first house. "The cattle on a thousand hills are mine for every animal of the forest is mine, and the cattle on a thousand hills. I know every bird in the mountains, and the insects in the fields are mine. If I were hungry, I would not tell you, for the world is mine, and all that is in it (Psalms 50:10-12)." David also said, "I have been young, and now am old; yet have I not seen the righteous forsaken, nor his seed begging bread (Palms 35: 25)." The word of God declares that my God shall supply all your needs according to his riches in glory in Christ Jesus our Lord (Philippians 4: 19) and I can do all things through Christ who strengthens me (Philippians 4:13).

I returned to Montego Bay with new zeal, new impetus, new life and new strength to fulfil my dream of having my own house. I was determined to save as much as I could, so I could start buying the blocks and steel I needed. I had made up my mind to go every single Monday morning to the National Commercial Bank in Montego Bay Parade to save my money, so I could have enough to go to Saint Elizabeth and buy the material I needed to start my house. By 1995, I started building my house in the same corner of land granddad gave to me.

My happiness was overshadowed at this time because I lost my beloved grandmother in late 1994. She suffered a massive stroke and passed away just three years after the passing of my mum. My grandmother, Mrs Hilda, was the dearest person on earth to me, after my mum. She came back to Jamaica from the UK, round about the time when I was born. I was told that I was a very pretty baby to look at, very fair, and my grandmother connected with me straightaway and loved me like her own child. She even nursed me with her breasts; I love my mother. I would sleep with her and my granddad and not with my mum. I was so close to her it was unbelievable she really loved me. I cannot say that I was the favourite but I was certainly loved by my grandmother, from the day I was born to the day she passed away, with a very special love.

Growing up she would give me special treatment, if for instance, she needed anything from the shops, she would call me, rather than her other grandchildren. I was the main one; I wasn't the eldest, nor was I the youngest, but she would call me. I was always willing to answer her call to say yes mama and I would run to her, and she would send me to the shops to buy things for her, knowing that I would run all the way to the shop and run back home with that old bike tyre that I pretended was my bicycle. I would run my tyre to the shops without stopping to play, without messing around and come straight back home. Sometimes she would whisper in my ear to buy a piece of tobacco for her. "But don't let your grandfather know!"

My grandfather who would either be in his room or out in the yard pulling up broom weed would hear exactly what my grandmother was saying because she was a bit deaf in her later years, so even when she whispered it was quite loud. My granddaddy let me know that he was cognizant of the conversation we were having, by clearing his throat. Then I'd make a sign to my grandmother not to say anything because my granddad was listening.

She'd always tell me to take 50 cents out of the money and buy myself something. I remember those days running to and from the shops in my local community; it was a really lovely, beautiful community. On the way to the shop, I'd shout out good morning to folks on the road and if I couldn't see some of the older people in their yards, I'd call out to them by name anyway. Then a voice would come back loud and clear from somewhere within because they knew it was me.

"Good morning my son, how is your grandmother doing? How is the rest of the family?"

I would let them know that all was well. And after they'd said:

"Say hello to your grandmother for me!"

I could go merrily along my way I would do that at each house. If I didn't, they would let my mum and my grandparents know:

"Your son passed here this morning and did not even say hello to me. He doesn't have any manners!"

I was known in the home to be a caring child. I even used to help my grandmother to walk to the toilet. I loved that lady so much; I would do anything for her. She was the Apple of my eye. In the mornings, she used to send me out to the lime bush tree so she could make bush tea for us before we went to school. Sometimes it was fever grass that we had to get for her, to make fever grass tea. She always took good care of us and I really loved her. It was so painful for me when she passed away when I was far away.

I came back from Montego Bay, knowing that my

grandmother would not be there anymore; it was a hard and painful journey. Since I became converted, every time I returned to Saint Elizabeth, I used to sit on the veranda with her and read the Bible to her. She had a big print Bible, given to her by her daughter, my auntie Lucy. I would read it to her and tell her about the love of God. She would cry and tell me about her commitment to God, how she loved God. I hope by God's grace that she has found a resting place in Jesus Christ our Lord.

It was hard for me to know that my grandmother was dead because as a little child growing up, whenever we had a funeral service in Spice Grove or Springfield and the hearse was passing the house, she would call out to us asking whose funeral it was. When I told her, she cried and cried and said she was afraid she would be next.

As children, we knew that our grandmother was really afraid of death; she did not want to die at all because she loved life. At the age of 74, she finally succumbed to a horrible stroke, which took her away from us. She was such a dear old lady, a kind and precious soul with a loving heart; she was one of the best grandmothers ever.

It was a painful journey from Montego Bay to Saint Elizabeth, about 70 miles away, knowing that I would never see her again. It was tough for me because I'd only lost my mum three years earlier in 1991. Now my grandmother followed her first child to be deceased. I remember the funeral service clearly. It was hard; it was really difficult for me. All my family members were crying and I was crying for my grandmother and my mother because it was a vivid reminder of the last time I was in the Hilltop Seventh-day Adventist Church, for my mother's funeral service. Now my grandmother was gone, the next dearest person to me on earth. I asked: "Why God? Why did you take her away from us, as we laid her to rest?"

I returned to Montego Bay, determined to work even harder to earn enough money to achieve my goal of making my house and coming back home. I had new zeal and energy and wanted to finish my house as quickly as possible. My grandmother wasn't there but at least my granddad was. Just three months later after laying our grandmother to rest in October 1994 by February 1995, I was in Montego Bay and heard the sad news that my granddad had passed away. How could this be? I'd just lost my mum four years earlier, my grandmother three months ago, how could my grandfather have died?

He was only 74, would have been 75 that year April the 3rd to be exact. He was strong and healthy and would walk 3 miles, every day back and forth, to do a little farming to keep himself active. He went every day except Sabbaths, very early in the mornings and came back at about 1 p.m. Then he cooked dinner for the family. He was so healthy and strong, unlike my grandmother who was very sickly for a long time, my granddad had never been ill. How could he have died, I questioned?

I was sadly informed that he had been over at his farm, looking after the land, taking care of his cows. He climbed a tree and sadly fell, knocking his head on a stone. He passed away instantly. When people found him there, they thought that maybe he was sleeping, but he had died. It was so sudden, without warning, the same age as my grandmother and just three months after her.

It was unbelievable; how could he have died? He hadn't even been very high up in the tree. He had given me the land to build my house on and I was so looking forward to his seeing me, his grandchild building that house but it wasn't meant to be. My granddad taught me everything I needed to learn from a man. With my father out of the picture, he became a father to me. He taught me how to be a good man, how to take care of a wife, how to love her even in difficult times, how to cook and clean for my wife and wash her clothes.

He was a good man. He would go to the shops, and he would do the shopping himself as a man. To this day I do the shopping and buy food, clothes anything we need and I learned all of that from my granddad. My granddad would not run out of anything; he would always have that extra buffer there if it was cooking oil, he would always have a little stashed away in his room. So, if we suddenly thought we were all out of cooking oil, he would go quietly into his room and give you what was needed. Then he would send us to the shops to get more.

On Fridays he went to Black River market, taking money from his pension. He spent many years working in the United Kingdom and had a good pension to show for it. He would always buy a nice piece of beef for Friday evening dinner, so we always knew we had beef soup for dinner. Saturday evenings we had salt fish and cabbage and on Sunday, chicken. He always made sure we had healthy food: red kidney beans; peas; it could be fish, just a tinned mackerel; God always provided something for us. My Grandfather was the one who taught me to save money. He said before I got married, I should have somewhere ready to live in with my wife.

I remember coming back to Saint Elizabeth and not only my mum and my grandmother but now my granddad too was dead. I prayed to God; I asked God, I said Lord when will this stop? If it continues this way, Lord, no one will be left alive in my family. I've been hard at work in Montego Bay, walking all over the rough hills of the most crime-infested areas, telling people about the love of God. Is this my reward, Lord, that the three people dearest to me are dead? Is this the result of serving you, Lord? Is this my reward for being faithful to you?

Hence, I could say like King David, when I look on the ungodly my feet almost slipped, because they do not serve God, but they appear to be flourishing and it appears as if all is going well with them (Psalm 73: 2-5). However, I was suffering so much, my family was just dying everywhere; I wondered when would it stop. At my grandfather's funeral, I was in tears; I was mourning for my grandfather but also my grandmother and my dear mother. Between 1991 and early 1995, three of the most precious people in my life had passed away; I wept I cried for them all.

The journey back to Montego Bay was a sad one. The first time had been after the passing of my mum, the second after the passing of my grandmother and now I was taking that journey after the passing of my grandfather. Who would be next? I asked myself.

At that time, I encouraged all my family members to put their trust and their confidence in God. I assured them that God is with us and God said to us: when you are going through the waters, I will be with you. When you are going through the fire, I will be with you. I will never leave you nor forsake you for the mouth of the Lord had spoken it (Isaiah 43: 1- 3). As I went back to Montego Bay, I was determined to have my house built by the following year, God willing. So, I worked hard, I saved hard and I made sacrifices. Finally, I started my first house in Saint Elizabeth, Little Bridge District. This was built on the same land that my grandfather gave me less than a year earlier. My dear mother, grandmother and grandfather were now all buried on the same land, as I started building a new home and a new life close to their resting place.

Finally, we started the groundwork. My Uncle Randolph was managing the project for me and I was told by the builders that I had to buy a chicken, kill it and sprinkle the blood on the land where I was going to build. I also had to get white rum and sprinkle it at the same spot, before the building could be started, otherwise the person who goes to live in that house might die. Now that I was converted and knew the word of God, I knew that all of these things were spiritualism. I was determined not to do it so I told them that I was so sorry, but I would not be killing a fowl, or buying any white rum. I would be moving into that house and I would not die but live and declare the word of the Lord (Psalm 118: 17). I believe that "except the LORD build the house, they labour in vain that build it: except the LORD keep the city, the watchman waketh but in vain. It is vain for you to rise up early, to sit up late, to eat the bread of sorrows: for so He giveth His beloved sleep" (Psalm 127). I was certain that God would take care of everyone who worked on the house and me; so far, all of us are still alive by God's grace.

The work started in earnest and I came down frequently, going to the hardware shop to get more building material and leaving it with my uncle. Finally, in 1996, the house was completed, to God be the glory. No more outside toilet when I came back home, because I now had my own toilet, indoors.

8

The Love of My Life

I remember meeting two beautiful young ladies and straight away we started talking. We kept talking and talking whenever we bumped into each other. Then one evening I was in Glendevon Seventh-day Adventist Church and people came from Harrison SDA Church because they were doing an exchange programme. I was sitting at the front of the church as usual, where I could be nearer to the preacher when this young lady came and sat behind me, during the evening programme and asked if she could have a look at my books.

I always took my briefcase to church with me every week. If I got into a discussion with anyone, I would take out the Spirit of Prophecy Books, which my aunt Lucy gave me; this was The Conflict of the Ages, a five-volume series. These books always accompanied me to church in my briefcase along with Early Writings, Last Days Events and my Bible. Whatever was going on, I could prove it from the word.

The young lady took a book from the bench and asked if she could borrow it. I said no problem at all because I was happy to introduce people to the service of God, so it was indeed a pleasure for me. I found it quite interesting that a young person had shown an interest in this type of book. I asked her if she knew what the book was about and if she knew its author? We discussed its merits and we chatted for quite a while until it was time to leave. I lived just down the road from the church so I said I was going home to change but would she be coming to the social later? To which she replied that she was.

When I came back in time for the social, I saw her there with other folks from Harrison Seventh-day Adventist Church and I was really keen to speak to her. Throughout the evening we stayed close to each other and she was my partner in many of the games, along with Alecia, her sister and another young lady I knew from before. There was no doubt in my mind exactly whom I wanted to start a relationship with and I asked her if she would come and see me at the barbershop, whenever she was free and happened to be in Montego Bay on Barnett Street? I gave her the address and told her that it is Oneness Plaza owned by the international singer and movie star Jimmy Cliff. I tried to keep the eagerness out of my voice, not to let on how much I wanted to see her.

The next day I kept looking out for her but she didn't come. I waited all week and never saw her. To say I felt disappointed was an understatement. I finally bumped into her again and asked why she hadn't turned up? She said she did come but when she didn't see me, she left. I begged her to come back another time. She said that when she realized where I worked, she didn't feel comfortable to visit me there, because all the barbers kept trying to chat her up and she didn't like that at all. In fact, she was rather surprised that I worked in such an environment.

I made sure I told everyone who she was so they didn't harass her anymore. Eventually, she started coming to visit me there, we got to know each other and the rest is history as they say. She was extremely disappointed when I told her of my intention to go back to Saint Elizabeth. We hadn't long known each other and the news came as something of a bombshell. She asked how long I would be staying away and I told her I was going back for good. I had built a house there and wanted to go back home to live, she was very unhappy. She was surprised that, as a young man of just 22, I would want to go back to the country, which seemed very backward compared to Montego Bay, a more progressive place with more opportunities.

She tried to persuade me not to return to Saint Elizabeth but my mind was made up. I did tell her though that I would be keeping in touch with her and I wasn't just running off and leaving her. I wanted to invite her to Saint Elizabeth one day, so she could come and visit and see my life there for herself. This certainly made her feel much better.

It was so hard telling everyone that I was moving back to Saint Elizabeth. I'd made so many friends in Montego Bay, so many people that I was close to. When I told the head elder (Elder Biggs) at Glendevon Church that I was leaving, it was really painful for both of us because we had developed such a good relationship during the time I lived in Glendevon and worshipped at the church, it was really tough.

He said he felt particularly sad because he had planned to step down as head elder after 7 years in the role. First of all, he had hoped another brother to be elder after him in Glendevon, but he moved away to Kingston to study. Then he had it in mind to suggest my name to the committee. I was shocked because I had never served as an elder; I was only 22 years old and Glendevon Church had a membership of over 1000 at the time. But he must have seen the work of God in my life for him to say that. Indeed, God had been working in my life in an amazing way from a very young age. God placed on me the burden of leadership and I love leading His people. This was "The incredible Dream".

My final day when I stood in Glendevon Church and it was announced that I was leaving, my heart sunk and I welled up with tears. It was tough for me to be leaving people that I'd come to love and appreciate and have had so many friendships with. My associates, while I was converted at Glendevon, were aged between 40 to 70 and we used to hang out together and talk about the Bible and the word of God, about the Spirit of Prophecy and prophecies, the coming of Christ, about final events and final times. We used to go deep. That was how I chose to spend my lunch break from church, instead of hanging out with guys of my own age. Some of these men had children my age while others even had grandchildren in their 20s and they were the people I preferred to hang out with, asking them questions and answering the difficult questions that they asked me. I believe they came to respect and appreciate me as an equal by the grace of God.

Also, I had some younger friends in Glendevon. I went to a campaign in Green Pond in 1993 and was invited by a young lady, called Trudy, to come to Glendevon Church. I was attending Mount Salem Church at the time because I'd just moved into the area. She encouraged me to come to Glendevon and introduced me to some of her friends. We are still friends to this day.

Just before I left Glendevon Church I preached my first sermon there. They gave me an evangelistic meeting to preach my first sermon which was about the giving of the law on Mount Sinai and the power of God coming down and meeting with his people and I went through all 10 commandments. I invited my fiancé, who is now my wife. She and her family came and I remember it was raining so hard that night, proper Caribbean rain but the family still came out to support me. I was so grateful for the support as I went up on the pulpit and preached my first ever sermon by the power of the Lord and God indeed was present that evening to confirm "The Incredible Dream".

I knew I had the gift of preaching long before, because when I was about 7 years old, God would be giving me sermons. He would just put sermons in my mind and I would think of all the great sermons that I could preach when I went to church and heard the preacher preaching. I would say wow, if I had the courage, I could preach so many things and it was as if God was just downloading sermons into my mind, from a very young age. I knew God has given me the gift of preaching. Not only that but in my everyday conversations with people, they would ask me if I was a preacher, long before I preached my first sermon. As God said to Jeremiah: I knew you from when you were in your mother's womb, from when you were conceived, I knew you from that time (Jeremiah 1:5). And I have called you and ordained you to be a preacher. So, I think God ordained me from birth to be a preacher; he laid on my heart to be a pastor and from a very early age, that's what I wanted to do.

Finally, everything was done and I'd informed everyone that I was definitely going back to Saint Elizabeth. People asked me if I had a job waiting for me there? I told them that God had blessed me with the house; my house is finished praise God. However, I hadn't got a job yet and I didn't know what I was going to do when I got there. But God had called me like Abraham and God had drawn me back to my hometown (Genesis12).

I had a dream about three years before that I should go back to Saint Elizabeth. God wanted me there and He had work for me to do in Saint Elizabeth. So, I told everyone I was just obeying the voice of God. I said to them, God will not take you where he cannot keep you, so I know "my God shall supply all my needs according to His riches in glory by Christ Jesus our Lord" (Philippians 4:19). I said to them the psalmist David said, "I was young and now I am old and I have never seen the righteous forsaken nor his seed begging bread" (Psalms 37: 25). I said to them it is a tough one but "I can do all things through Christ who strengthens me" (Philippians 4:13). I said don't worry, pray for me I'm well able to capture this land, anywhere with Jesus, I can safely go anywhere he leads me in this world (Helen C. Alexander). And I was happy to leave the city because I wasn't really a city boy. I'd rather live in the countryside, to feel the fresh breeze blowing and hear the birds singing.

I left Montego Bay and thanks to Brother Mackenzie, I was privileged to use his van to take all my belongings and me safely to Saint Elizabeth. God had provided me with a house but no work and no money except what I had with me. There was no-one there any more whom I could depend upon for money, except God. My Grandfather whom I used to depend on was dead, my mother, my grandmother who used to give me money from time to time, had died. My auntie Dora who sustained me in Montego Bay many times when I was hungry, she was such a kind lady to me, she had also died just months before I returned home at the end of 1995. I attended her funeral service and then went back to Montego Bay.

Now, I was home in Saint Elizabeth with no help and no support, except the full trust and confidence in the Lord, that God had led me back to Saint Elizabeth and He would keep me because the word of God says, "I will keep him in perfect peace, whose mind is stayed on me" (Isaiah 26:3). So, I felt calm and composed and praised God. "I will bless the LORD at all times: his praise shall continually be in my mouth. My soul shall make her boast in the LORD: the humble shall hear thereof, and be glad. O magnify the LORD with me, and let us exalt his name together. I sought the LORD, and he heard me, and delivered me from all my fears" (Psalm 34: 1-3).

Feeling calm and comfortable, I sorted my clothes out and on the following day, went outside and did a bit of washing to make sure my clothes were clean. I started unpacking everything and then cooked a vegan meal, spoke to my friends and went for a stroll to enjoy the fresh air. It all felt so beautiful and refreshing and it was so good to know that I was no longer in Montego Bay. I had worked in a rough part of Montego Bay, sandwiched between Hart Street and Barnett Lane. Sometimes fighting would break out between the two rival gangs and the place would be littered with broken bottles, stones and knives. Now, after such a rough environment, I was finally home in my quiet country environment and God has provided for me my own home. I could now say 'home sweet home' and I felt really happy.

In September 1996, I relocated. I had touched base with my relatives and was enjoying the environment. I made sure everything was clean and when I went to bed that night, I prayed to God. Did I have a job? No, I didn't have work. Was I worried? No, I wasn't worried at all because I knew that God would provide something for me. I had two skills; I could easily go back to my cabinet-making which I had been doing years before. I could make furniture, such as beds, tables and chairs. There were at least three cabinet-maker shops in the community and others in Black River, so I could go back to doing that. Plus, I had been a senior barber in Montego Bay, the second city of Jamaica, so it shouldn't be difficult for me to pick up a job in Black River.

The following morning, I got nice and clean and fresh; at 22 years old, I told my folks that I was going to Black River to look for a job as a Barber. When I got there, I bumped into some folks I hadn't seen for years. One of them was an old schoolmate from Pondside School and she told me there was a barber's shop opposite the police station. Apparently, four barbers had left recently so the owner was looking to take on more staff.

I thanked her and headed on down there. It turned out to be the very same shop where I used to have my hair cut as a boy and for my graduation 5 years earlier. I met the original Barber, who had allegedly been the first to open a barber's shop in that part of Saint Elizabeth. He remembered me from all those years ago. I explained that I had come back home to live, I had worked as a barber for 4 years in Montego Bay and I would be interested in a job with him. He asked if I could start tomorrow and I assured him I could. However, I quickly informed him I was a Seventh-day Adventist Christian and it was non-negotiable about working on the Sabbath, I could not work on Saturdays, ever.

He assured me he had no problem with that at all. Then he showed me my chair and we went through the different procedures. I accepted gladly and so from going down to Saint Elizabeth with no work and finding a job straight away, who could it be but God, who had that job ready for me? God Himself lined it up, not me.

I quickly got involved in all the services at my home church, Hilltop SDA. I went to Wednesday night prayer meetings, Sunday night evangelistic meetings and Sabbath services. Very soon they started asking me to lead out in Wednesday night prayer meetings, Sunday night meetings and Sabbath services, not only to preach but to do Bible class and before long I was doing everything in the church, from lesson study to preaching, to Bible class. In the same year, 1996, I was asked to be an elder in the church at the age of 22 and not just an elder but the head elder. This was the church that I grew up in. My mum went to this church, grandfather and other relatives, they all came here and now I was asked to be the head elder at the age of 22, to lead these people I'd grown to love and to respect.

Then the pastor came to see me.

"Otis," he said. "The members of the nomination committee have asked you to be the head elder of the church. I said to them you can't be the head elder because you have never served in an office before and you have just come back from Montego Bay. So, I had the whole voting process repeated and I asked everyone to vote again for a new head elder. Unanimously they voted for you again, even though I told them not to vote for you because it is not ideal for you to be the head elder; you have never held the office of an elder before. Therefore, I'm asking you kindly if you could just allow someone else to serve as a head elder for this year because the nomination committee is determined not to use anyone else but you as the head elder." This was a glimpse of "The Incredible Dream"

I gladly gave it up and said I was willing to serve in any capacity. I'd only served officially as an usher in this same church and never had another office in the church. When I was informed that my name would have been put forward to be the head elder in Glendevon, with over 1,000 members, I turned it down because I was going back to Saint Elizabeth to live. So, I did not hold office in Glendevon Church, even though I was very active there.

In January of the following year, 1997 I informed the board under the then pastor, that I would like to do a revival. I was so surprised to see the number of people who turned up to the revival at the church. People were standing outside and they had come from all over the area. To be honest, I was terrified. I hadn't expected so many people but they had heard that there's a new preacher, come back from Montego Bay. When I left the community, I could hardly talk; I was one of the quietest people in the community and now I was a loudmouth preacher, by the grace of God. I preached about the love of God and the power of God during the crucifixion of Christ, Hallelujah! That night the church was filled with the power of the Holy Spirit. The Holy Spirit arrested and impelled me to preach His word with power (Jeremiah 20:9). The Bible says, "wait at Jerusalem until you have received the Holy Spirit from on high when you have received the Holy Spirit you should be witnesses for me both in Jerusalem, Judea in Samaria and to the utmost parts of the world" and indeed I was a mouthpiece for God (Acts 1: 6, 8). That night I remember clearly when the Spirit of God presented the word of God through me in form of crucifixion, they were crying, they were weeping tears and the spirit of God led many people to the altar. I remember one lady, a teacher and a very quiet lady, not the Hallelujah type, not the person that sits in the "amen corner", but she came down to the alter walking on her knees, shouting praises to God and the Spirit of God rested heavily upon her, the Spirit of God indeed truly was in that place and many people were prepared for baptism.

That revival was my first and my fiancé, who is now my wife, came to support me, as did my aunt from Lacovia and my aunt from America as well. They were all there supporting me, during that revival series. It was so powerful and the church was revived by the grace of God. Many people, who had stopped coming to church, started coming back. People in the community seemed to believe that a new John the Baptist was in town but I give God all the praise and glory. People from other churches were asking, who is this new preacher we have heard about? When they were told I was from the community and had grown up there, they were so happy to meet me.

I would lead the church in fasting and prayer on one Tuesday in each month. On one of these solemn occasions, the Spirit of God rested heavily on all of us in the service. After a season of prayer, three doves flew inside the church and lingered in the building for a while. The doves then flew around cheerfully and made their exit through each of the three doors, as opposed to all leaving by one door together.

9

Marriage to the Beautiful Marsha, 1997

In January of the same year, I remember Aunt Cherry getting married and I was privileged to be one of the officiating ministers at the wedding ceremony in the Black River Seventh-day Adventist Church. All the time, I was thinking about my own wedding coming up. This was the precursor and encouraged me to go forward and make the move to get married to my beautiful fiancé. I was really happy for the privilege to play the part that my aunt allowed me to minister.

By the time this book is published, Marsha will have been my beautiful wife for 23 precious years. When she was still my fiancée, she used to visit me in Saint Elizabeth and stay for the weekend, or even sometimes for a week and it was on one of those occasions that I proposed to her. I thought it might not be as fancy as for instance, proposing in a TV program, but trust me it doesn't matter where you propose, the important thing is love. What is the point of proposing on TV and then the following year, you are separated?

I remember sitting her down and speaking to her about my commitment, how I wanted to commit my life to her, not just for time but for eternity, for better or worse, in sickness and in health until death do us part. I'd waited for six years since my mum passed away. I wanted to find someone to be mine, someone whom I could share my life with. I was overjoyed when she said yes, I will marry you.

We did not have a massive wedding, but our relatives and friends came and it was the happiest day of my life. I had been waiting for something like this for so long. Six years ago, I had felt such sorrow after the passing of my mum, grandparents and my auntie and now it was time for some happiness. I was overjoyed to be marrying my young bride. We've had the most wonderful, marriage, growing together, creating a family together, blessed with wonderful children. I remember coming up to the wedding day, it was stressful, making sure everything was ready. But by the grace of God, the Lord came through and everything was finally ready.

We spent our honeymoon in Lacovia, such an enjoyable time; I cherish every moment of it, spending the rest of the week that I was off, as newlyweds. I loved this young Marsha so much and she loved me too. We were madly in love with each other; there was nothing we wouldn't do for each other. She would give the world for me and I would give even more for her. After we got married, my wife got a job at the Black River Dental Clinic. With both of us working, it made life much easier.

At that time, I was very active in the church. As well as serving as head Elder, I was ordained as an elder in 1998. It was a privilege to serve as the district representative of the Lay Preachers' League. I then became the chaplain of the Lay Preachers' League in Saint Elizabeth, in charge of organizing and arranging all the lay preaching that took place in the entire parish of Saint Elizabeth. I was in charge of arranging preachers for week of prayer, revivals and lay campaign. We used to travel all over the parish and also go to Santa Cruz Seven-day Adventist Church for 3 pm, where we had a meeting every month. It was a grand time, very active and very involved. I was busy doing funeral services, week of prayer, revivals, campaigns all over the place. "The Incredible Dream" was still alive.

I was preaching in many different places when a pastor sent for me in 2001 to do a campaign in Middle Quarters, Saint Elizabeth. He said that the Personal Ministry Director form the West Jamaica Conference in Montego Bay had recommended me. They sent a pastor all the way to Saint Elizabeth; the preacher he had previously arranged for his campaign was unable to fulfil his commitment, so the Personal Ministry Leader sent him to me saying he was sure I could fulfil that duty, with just four days' notice. This was on a Wednesday and the campaign was due to start on Sunday. I needed to give all my sermon titles for 24 sermons and everything in by Thursday, for them to print the handbill on Friday. It was tough but I decided to accept. That was my last campaign in Saint Elizabeth and Jamaica. We moved to Mandeville that same month because my wife was due to start a degree in education at West Indies College or Northern Caribbean University as it was then.

It was very difficult for us to move from my hometown; I had lived there from 1996 until 2001 but now it was time for me to move on because my wife was going to be studying in Mandeville. By then, I had my own business in Saint Elizabeth, a barbershop. I had at least one person working with me at the time. To give up my business and everything and go to Mandeville, not knowing what God would provide for us in terms of job, or in terms of business was hard. However, I knew I was going there to support my wife and at some time during her studies, I would start my own degree in Theology, as a pastor, which showed that "The Incredible Dream" was still alive and thriving.

I knew it would be challenging but I also believed that God

would not take you where he cannot keep you. We rented a house in Mandeville, quite a distance from the university and with not a very good water supply, something I wasn't used to at all. We had to travel down to Mandeville and back up again, taking my wife to University and for me to go to work in the morning. She was working and studying while I worked at the Willow Gate Plaza as a barber, which I did from September to December.

Marsha completed her first semester in December with great success. I asked her sister, Alecia to stay with her in Mandeville for me, while I finished up the campaign. Things were tough in Mandeville. We didn't have much money and there was the University fee to be paid. I didn't have many clients as a barber but we were determined to continue to plough on through. I had given up leadership, after being head elder for many years and we were now in Mandeville for the long haul, at least that's what we thought.

After living in Mandeville for four months, it was now time for us to move on to greener pastures but one of my church brothers (Brother Anderson) whom I had met recently, said he would give me an invitation to go to the United Kingdom. I was so delighted. I was so happy since no-one had been willing to give me an invitation to the United Kingdom before, even though I had so many family members living there. I called Brother Anderson and informed him that I would love to visit for the Christmas holiday. He said to no problem at all my brother. I was thrilled and so excited.

I started making plans to go to the United Kingdom. I tried to get some money from my dad and relatives abroad, to see if anyone was willing and able to make up my aeroplane fare. Unfortunately, there was no one abroad who would assist me in this trip. I decided to look locally. I spoke to my wife's sister, Alecia and my cousin, Richard and they agreed they would make up the shortfall for my airfare and spending money for the United Kingdom. I thanked them both for their generosity and their willingness to support me.

I booked my flight, leaving Jamaica on 19th December, arriving in the United Kingdom on Thursday, December 20th. Then on Friday, 14th of December, I became unwell with an extremely high temperature. After a sleepless night, I was unable to go to church on the Sabbath and by Sunday, I found myself at the Mandeville Hospital. When the nurse in charge saw me lying down in my wife's lap, groaning with pain, she came over and asked about my symptoms. I explained that I had a high temperature, which wasn't going down, and I was in a lot of pain.

She told us we were about twentieth in the queue but she would take me in next because she could see I needed urgent attention. I did not have the words to thank her for her kindness. Then after she called me in, the doctors diagnosed me with chickenpox. I was relieved to know that it was only that and not something far worse. However, it was still uncomfortable and I was in a lot of pain.

I told the doctor that I should be going to the United Kingdom on Wednesday; my flight was booked and everything, could I still go? They said absolutely not. No way could I get on a plane; I should cancel my flight because it was not safe for me to travel, not only because I was so unwell but also my Chickenpox was very contagious at that time. So, in the end, I cancelled my flight to the United Kingdom and re-booked it for 25th December, Christmas Day. I would arrive there on Boxing Day.

The night before flying, I stayed at my wife's family's house, because they lived in Montego Bay. They all came to the airport to see me off. I had packed my suitcase well, with clothes ready for the winter weather. I was well-dressed in a suit and jacket, determined not to be caught out by the cold which everybody had warned me about. I was well prepared, with a string vest, a T-shirt, a shirt and my jacket, more than enough for the winter in my opinion. Little did I know how cold it was in the UK.

I remember walking out onto the tarmac, waving goodbye to my wife and her family and climbing aboard the plane bound for Miami. In those days, people could watch you going across the tarmac and if you got a window seat, you might be able to see your relatives waving. It was my third time in an aeroplane, so I wasn't as petrified as two years ago when I had travelled to Barbados for the Festival of the Laity.

I enjoyed this flight and in less than two hours, we had landed in Miami. Security was exceptionally tight at the airport. Remember this was only four months after 9/11 and the guards had sniffer dogs out and everything. Finally, by the grace of God, we went through transit in Miami and connected to our flight to the United Kingdom. Again, I really enjoyed my ride.

We reached Heathrow Airport at approximately 7 in the morning and landed safely by the grace of God. Now it was time for the next hurdle. I had to pass through immigration control. I had been told so much about the problems people faced here when trying to enter the United Kingdom, with many of them being turned back at the airport. I remember thinking of the embarrassment that would cause and the anxiety about what would happen with the money that I borrowed? I would have to work so hard to pay all of that back. Worst of all, I would be going back in a disgraceful manner, back to Mandeville, back to my workplace.

When the immigration officer spoke to me, he seemed concerned about the spots on my face but I quickly informed him that I had suffered from chickenpox over two weeks ago; it was over now and the doctors had assured me that I was safe to travel and not contagious at all. He asked me a few more questions, then said I was free to enter the country. I knew my brothers Anderson and Andrew would be there to meet me, so no more problems for me to cope with. God had proven Himself great once again.

However, after walking out of Immigration Control and into the Arrivals Hall, I found no-one there to meet me. In fact, I had to wait over an hour before they arrived. I was surprised because we're always being told that only people in the Caribbean are late and don't know the time but when you're in England, America or Canada, no-one is ever late. At least I felt happy that I'd made it into the country.

I didn't have a mobile phone, unlike everyone else in the waiting area. I saw a Jamaican guy and asked him if I could please call someone on his phone? I had Brother Anderson's mobile number and also his landline. He was happy to lend me his phone and when I managed to speak to Brother Anderson, he told me that they were on their way but running a bit late. I said it was no problem at all and I looked forward to seeing them.

Finally, they arrived and gave me the bad news. I would not be able to stay with my uncle as we had arranged, because he said that things had changed. There was nowhere for me to stay and they would have to send me back to Jamaica. He didn't want to do that to me but he said where he lived wasn't suitable. This was why they'd been late coming to pick me up at the airport.

This was the first time I had met Brother Andrew but I had heard a lot about him.

"When I look at you," he said. "I can see God in you. Oh, truly that you are a child of God and I'm going to help you. You can stay with me."

He explained that he lived in sheltered accommodation, which he had only just moved into in October. As the new kid on the block, he didn't want to rock the boat. However, he would let the people there know that I would be staying with him for a short time.

I was so tired. I had no idea this had been going on while I was in the air. Now I was confronted by all this new information and changes of plan. I didn't know what was happening but surely God said, I will not leave you nor forsake you (Hebrews13: 5). I will be with you always even until the end of the age (Matthew 28:20). I knew God was providing a way through for me because He had work for me to do in the United Kingdom.

I really enjoyed that first evening in the United Kingdom, despite being so tired it was unbelievable. I had a nice dinner with Brother Anderson and his wife Sister Merna. Roxroy who came to see me had only arrived here himself about six months before me. We had a good talk it was great to see him after six months.

God started providing for me from that very day onwards. I eventually enrolled in college and applied for further leave to remain in the United Kingdom. I enjoyed my time in the United Kingdom. My greatest heartache, however, was that my wife was not with me. I missed her so much and I called her every single day. I didn't have the facilities for Skype. Therefore, I had to buy a calling card each time but I always called her without fail every single day.

10

Reunion December 2002

I had been in the UK for nearly a year, phoning my wife every day to see how she was doing and let her know how much I loved her and cared for her, that she was the cherry on my cake and the honey in my tea. She was nearly 6,000 thousand miles and just a heartbeat away. My love for her was as bright now as ever and it was just a matter of time before God would reunite us and I could love and care for her and by God's grace, I would never leave her again.

It was hard trying to enjoy living in a cold country without my wife. Life was challenging, it was tough and difficult but I knew that God would see us through and it was only a matter of time before we would be reunited. They say absence makes the heart grow fonder but it was tough being apart from the one I loved so dearly. We had been married for four years and now spending almost a year apart.

It wasn't the first time we'd been apart. Two years into our marriage, in 1999, I had to go abroad to the Festival of the Laity in Barbados, which was only for only four days. Four days was clearly not the same as a year. I was a young man and waking up in the morning, I longed to see the most precious person in the world lying next to me.

Each month it became more difficult to live apart from her. It was tough holding on for such a long time. There were many young ladies in the church but I was determined to hold on and to be true to my marriage vows. Finally, December came and it was now God's time for us to be together in the United Kingdom.

We were singing and praising God all the way to the airport, some powerful hymns such as 'We Are Nearing Home' and 'Master The Tempest'. I waited in the terminal building and the plane had landed. I looked at everyone coming in from that flight. I would trust God like Job, though He slays me yet will I trust Him (Job 13: 15) and I know my Redeemer lives and in the end I shall see Him for myself and not another (Job 19: 25). So, I trusted God and placed my confidence in God. Additionally, we were truly grateful to Sister Merna who gave my wife the invitation.

I stood there, waiting and waiting and waiting. I hadn't seen my wife in a whole year. I waited with bated breath. I looked at everyone who turned the corner to see if it was her; how would she look? She must have changed a bit. I changed also. I was extremely slim when I came to the United Kingdom but now in this country, I had put on some weight. So, if I looked different, how would she look? I wasn't even sure what to expect. Technology wasn't as it is now where we have Facebook and WhatsApp and so on so we never had the opportunity to see each other speaking from across the world in those days.

At last, turning the corner came the most beautiful young lady in the world. We were both in our 20s at the time and she was stunning to look at. There she was, grinning from ear to ear, she couldn't wait to hold me and neither could I wait to hold her and tell her how much I loved her. Finally, she came through the barrier into the arrivals hall and I grabbed her, hugged her and lifted her up off the ground. I told her I would never leave her again and that we would be forever together by the grace of God. I was so happy, so delighted that my wife and I were united once more after such a long time apart.

We headed for the car and drove home to the place, which would become her home for the next 20 years. That night was a night I shall never forget, a special night. God is truly amazing; it was worth the wait, truly it was worth the wait. My wife was finally with me; nothing could go wrong now. All our prayers had been answered.

Not long after she arrived in the UK, she was expecting our first baby, Rachel. This coincided with the time when she was preparing herself, keeping fit, going out jogging each morning, because her plan was to be a nurse in the British Army, at least that's what we thought. Not long after it was discovered that she was pregnant and when we did that test and it came out positive, we were so excited. We had been married for five years and for one of those years we had been apart and now she was expecting our first baby.

It was a very exciting time and we worked together to take care of our new baby because she had never been pregnant before and we weren't sure how this pregnancy would go. She was quite young, so we felt sure there would be no problems at all. However, to our surprise from the word go, my wife was sick. Some ladies have morning sickness, but she had all-day and all-night sickness. It seemed as if my wife couldn't eat or keep down anything at all. I wondered how she was going to cope and what would happen to her? Would she be able to go through this when she was so unwell? Then finally she seemed to be getting a little stronger and the sickness started to go away. We had passed the first trimester. I remember going to look at the baby, the little foetus moving around. I remember all the clinics and the appointments we had with the GP. I would take time off and attend all of those appointments with my wife, making sure we were together.

I supported her all the way and eventually, we started to relax because the pregnancy got much better and my wife was now OK. She wasn't throwing up as much as before and we could enjoy the pregnancy as opposed to being worried about everything. One Friday evening, I received a call from my wife: please come fast, I think I am in labour. I thought no Lord, that can't be possible it was too soon, too early. I made my way quickly to the Lewisham Hospital and went straight into the room where the midwife was with my wife. I asked her how my wife was and she assured me she was alright. However, when I asked about the baby, she said they couldn't give us any guarantees. Then my wife went into labour.

I didn't know what I could do to help. My wife was crying in pain and they had given us a side room because they knew the prognosis was not good. After about four hours, the midwife was called back into the room and she delivered the baby. I had asked the nurse earlier if my wife was going to die, she was in so much pain. She said your wife should be alright but the baby might not make it. When the midwife delivered the baby, she said she resembled her dad, she's the spitting image of her daddy.

I remember my wife holding our daughter and being told that sadly, she would not make it. It was a tough time for us to finally leave her there. We stayed overnight and on the Sabbath we went home. We had no energy, no strength. We locked ourselves away in our room, not wanting to come out nor see anyone, nor answer any questions. We were devastated, knowing that our first child was now in the morgue. It was tough leaving her there while we went home and to add insult to injury, it was our anniversary weekend that Friday the 8th and our anniversary on Sunday 10th of August 2003.

The following two weeks were hard to endure. The nurses told us that we could come back and see our little baby and we gladly accepted the opportunity to see her, between the birth and the funeral. I shall never forget the nurses sending us to look about arranging for a birth certificate and a death certificate. Most new parents would be cheerfully arranging for the birth certificate of their child, but for us, it was a death certificate. It was a terrible time for us.

The day of the funeral, we gathered at Hither Green Crematorium. All I could think of was our dear baby, Rachel Lewis. We were so grateful for the support of our family and friend, that we had Brother Lewis and Della with us, especially as the coffin was brought inside and as they lay it gently inside the crematorium, our hearts broke and my wife and I were crying inconsolably. They offered us comfort at this painful time but it seemed like nothing could ease our grief; we had lost our precious baby girl and we would never see her again until when Jesus comes the second time.

We were crying uncontrollably, the tears just kept coming as my little baby lay there for the time that we were given by the crematorium. We had considered cremation as the better of two evils because the other option of burial my wife said would be too difficult for her to stand and watch over her little baby being buried.

After the preacher finished, he tried to encourage us by telling us about the love of God. By this time, I was in my late 20s and I had performed many funeral services myself. However, there was no funeral service like this one. I had no strength to do this one. I had been an ordained elder for over five years and I was well-established in many funeral services, laying people to rest. Nonetheless, it was different when my dear beloved Rachel was laid to rest when the minister finished his discourse and was about to lay my beloved daughter to rest. It was sudden, it was cold, it was brutal after doing the committal and then he lowered my daughter silently and quickly with no prior warning. I had the opportunity to do several cremation services at this same crematorium and made an effort to inform and prepare the family of the deceased before I pressed the button to lower the coffin.

I wanted to grab that tiny coffin. I wanted to pull her back, to take her out. I wanted to take her home. I wanted her to come and be at her home where she truly belonged and keep her. I wanted her to be mine, to be ours forever, to hug her, to love her, keep her, kiss her to feed and nourish her. She was our first child, our daughter; we wanted to do everything for her. We wanted to hear her cry, hear her first cry. We wanted her to cry like any other baby. We wanted to change her nappy, put her in bed, take her out of bed. We wanted her to wake us up in the night, to give us sleepless nights. We wanted to prepare her feed, to cool her feed. We wanted her to suck her mother's breast. We wanted to push her in her own pushchair. We wanted her to get her own space in this world, it wasn't fair for her to be just born and then pass away. What had we done to deserve this? Was it a punishment? Why was God punishing us like this? Why did we lose our baby, Rachel?

Then my mind turned to the scripture, which says, all things work together for the good of those who are called, according to His purpose and I know we are called by God (Romans 8: 28). I knew that somehow good would come from this and my mind went forward to the resurrection when I would see my dear, beloved Rachel again (1 Thessalonians 4: 16 - 18).

Jesus declares that I am the resurrection and the life, he that believes in me, though he was dead, yet shall he live again, (John 11: 25 & 26). The Lord said, Gather my saints together unto me, those who have made a covenant with me by sacrifice, (Psalm 50: 5). Ellen White said, "The living righteous are changed 'in a moment, in the twinkling of an eye' (1 Corinthians 15: 52). At the voice of God, they were glorified; now they are made immortal, and with the risen saints are caught up to meet their Lord in the air. Angels "gather together His elect from the four winds, from one end of heaven to the other." Little children are borne by holy angels to their mothers' arms. Friends long separated by death are united, nevermore to part, and with songs of gladness ascend together to the city of God" (The Great Controversy, p.645, 1911). She saw those Angels taking the babies and placing them in their family group, placing them back with their mother and their father, placing them in the arms of their parents again. For those babies who had no parents in heaven because their parents did not make it, for one reason or another, then for those babies Adam and Eve would be their parents because the truth be told, they are the first parents, so they would be the parents for the children who do not have any parents who have made it to heaven to the Kingdom of God.

"For the Lord himself shall descend from heaven with a shout, with the voice of the archangel, and with the trump of God: and the dead in Christ shall rise first: Then we which are alive *and* remain shall be caught up together with them in the clouds, to meet the Lord in the air: and so shall we ever be with the Lord. Wherefore comfort one another with these words" (1 Thessalonians 4: 16- 18).

It's the Apostle Paul who tells us that death is swallowed up in victory: Oh, death where is your sting, oh grave where is your victory? The sting of death is sin and the strength of sin is a law, death will be no more (1 Corinthians 15: 54 - 56). We laid our dear, beloved Rachel to rest and then we walked out of that place back to an empty home, a home without our new-born baby, for whom we had such great plans but God had other plans for her. (Revelation 14: 13; Psalm 116: 15).

Much later we went back to the Hither Green Crematorium in London's Lewisham and placed an order for a little plaque for our baby, with the name Rachel Lewis, love Mum, Dad and Sister. Further on it would become Love Mum and Dad and sisters, all the other sisters that God has blessed baby Rachel with and we placed the plaque on Rachel's stone in Hither Green Crematorium where it stays to this day, precious in the sight of the Lord is the death of his saints and indeed she was precious and is still precious and will always be precious in the sight of the Lord (Psalm 116: 15).

Now we look forward to the day when the Lord Himself shall descend from heaven with a shout and will call our baby Rachel back and will present us in family groups again and give us our precious baby back. We'll hold her tight forever and there we shall be with the Lord forever. In Revelation, we were told that there's a group of 144 thousand and they followed the lamb wheresoever he goes (Revelation 14: 4). The servant of God declares that "I saw the little ones climb, or, if they chose, use their little wings and fly, to the top of the mountains and pluck the never-fading flowers." (Early Writings by Ellen G. White, p. 19). One day there will be peace in the Valley, one day there'll be no more sickness, no more death, no more pain, no more crying for the former things will be passed away and behold all things are become as new (Revelation 21:1- 7).

11

Computer Studies 2002-2005

By 2005, I had done several courses in computer studies and enrolled in various colleges. I enjoyed these courses. I wasn't computer-literate so it was a privilege for me to study this subject. I was working and studying at the same time and I met many new friends, some of whom I am still in touch with to this day.

I was also very active in church, taking part in many different activities. I worked within the Personal Ministry Department, in the Brixton Seventh-day Adventist Church. By now I had transferred my membership from Jamaica to the Brixton Seventh-day Adventist Church, one of the biggest of its kind in Europe and that's where my membership remains to this day. I later served as an elder there for approximately 10 years. I had a good relationship with all the elders but specifically Elders D.H Clarke and Moody, whose kindness and support I shall never forget. Sister Norton remembers our children's birthdays and our anniversary without fail to this day of which we are grateful.

I prayed about which direction I should take in terms of my degree studies. I wanted to do theology all along but I kept putting it off because it was too expensive. I had to wait until I had saved enough money to go to Newbold College to study theology. So finally, I decided that I would be going to do my theological course in Newbold by the grace of God. Moses was facing the Red Sea and on both sides were mountains (Exodus 14). I had no other way out but for God to say to me, stand still and see the Salvation of the Lord, for the enemy you see today you shall see no longer (Exodus 14: 13). Hence, after a discussion with my wife, I decided that I would be enrolled at Newbold College.

I went on the Internet to check them out first and then I called them up to tell them about my intention to start the course with them in September 2005. I told them which qualifications I had acquired to date and they invited me to come in and bring all my details, which I did. I was rejoicing because finally, I would be fulfilling my God-given calling, my call to gospel ministry to be a minister, this is "The Incredible Dream". With my back against the wall, God had decided that now was the time for me to study. Enough of these short courses, enough of my comfort zone, the time had come for me to prove myself and be tested. The Lord said, "Prove me now and see if I will not open up the windows of heaven and pour you out a blessing" (Malachi 3: 10). The Lord challenged me and said, you have been preaching for years about having faith, now it's your time to exercise your faith in Me, your trust in Me. I will take you through Newbold and when you finish with Newbold you will be debt-free. I am able, I am God, "I am the God of Abraham, Isaac and Jacob" (Exodus 3: 6). Jesus is the same yesterday, today and forevermore (Hebrews13: 8). You have heard the testimonies of pastors who have gone to college to study and who never knew where the next penny was coming from but I have supplied their needs. It is time for you to trust Me and to know that I will supply your needs as well. You are my child and I said to you "I have loved you with an everlasting love and with loving kindness I have drawn you unto me" (Jeremiah 33: 3). Remember I said you are "the apple of my eyes" (Zachariah 2: 8), the psalmist says "I have been young and now I am old and I have never seen the righteous forsaken nor his seed begging bread" (Psalm 37: 25). Consequently, how will you be begging bread by going to Newbold College? You will not be begging bread; you will be the head and not the tail (Deuteronomy 28: 13).

I enrolled in Newbold and travelled up with Brother Salmon, now Pastor Salmon. He was kind enough to give me a lift in his car and we did that whenever we both had classes on the same day, otherwise I would take the train from Clapham Junction to Bracknell and walk approximately two miles up to Newbold College. I was told that I had to start with the access year and then the following year I would do my first year in Bachelor of Divinity (BD). I wanted to study so badly that this did not deter me at all. My calling was to be a minister of religion, a pastor so I would not be put off by having to complete an access year. I enrolled and everything went well by the grace of God. I was very committed and I never missed any class time, travelling back and forth from London to Newbold College, studying, and submitting my coursework on time, being present for my exams and doing well. I was eager to learn.

The first semester came and went in no time. I felt as if I was locked away in a convent because the entire world appeared to be standing still. I remember over that Christmas holiday, planning that in January 2006 I would be going back to Newbold to complete my final semester and then finally I would be enrolled on the BD program. I enjoyed the Christmas holiday with my wife, family, friends and church. By then we had been at Good News Branch Sabbath School where we were leaders, which we had left Brixton earlier that year in April 2005 to establish. Eighteen of us left Brixton and went to York Gardens Library and Community Centre, to form a new church. We formed that church on steady foundations, the rock of Jesus

Christ. The church was going on wonderfully and I was doing my Revelation series on a weekly basis. We were preaching and getting people involved. Visitors came to our church from all over, to be blessed. I worked hard in the church over that holiday and also enjoyed time with my family.

In January, one bright clear Monday morning, I went to Newbold with Brother Michael; both of us were excited to be paying our school fees. I had the money, which I had earned over the holiday period and everything was ready for me to return to Newbold, to continue my studies for my college degree in theology to fulfil "The Incredible Dream". I went to the academic services to get my grades and discovered they were much better than expected. All that hard work and studying for so long had paid off, my grades were brilliant for the subjects that I did. I had mainly B pluses, B and one C plus. When I looked at my transcript, I was very pleased.

Academic Services informed me that I needed to go and see the person in charge of my year, the Year Coordinator. However, to my surprise, when I sat down in a meeting with this lecturer, he told me my results were not good enough for me to continue on the course. They had been looking for much higher grades and unfortunately; they couldn't keep me on the theology course. On top of this, they thought I was a home student. Because I was an international student that meant they would have to give me a letter to take to the Home Office, which just added to my dilemma.

I begged them; I beseeched and pleaded with them to let me finish the year at least. I said I have one B, 2 B plusses and 1 C plus, which should be enough to carry me on the course. However, they said if this was what I achieved now when I got to the BD course, they didn't believe I would be able to manage it. I said please give me a chance to prove myself. I will be able to manage the BD course, I insisted but they said, unfortunately, we are not able to keep you at Newbold.

It was a hard time for me, a challenging time. What would I say to my wife? She knew I had gone the college with the money to enrol, now I would have to go back and tell her that I had not been accepted at Newbold with the grades I had. To be honest, I could not understand because if the passing grade was C and I had all the passing grades, I could not understand why I should be dropped off the course. If I had failed my courses then that would be a different story but now I'd passed everything, this was tough. I could not explain it, neither could I understand it. I had my school fee why wasn't I allowed to continue on this course?

Finally, I realized that they weren't going to let me stay on at the college and I left with a heavy heart and tears in my eyes. "The Incredible Dream" had just died; at least that's how I felt. I walked off the Newbold campus with nowhere else to turn since this was the only Seventh-day Adventist Academy in the United Kingdom. I wasn't ready to go back to Jamaica; my hopes of becoming a pastor were dashed. Could it be that God was showing me signs that He did not want me to be a pastor? Should I call it a day? What would I do?

I walked away from Newbold that day wounded with tears in my eyes and a broken heart, and I was a broken man. This was my dream, I really wanted to be a minister of religion and I thought that I was not even given a fair chance. Not knowing what would happen, I went back to London. It was a bitter and hard pill to swallow but I took my pill and swallowed it without any water then I went home. When Marsha, my wife came in from work, I told her the news, that unfortunately, I would not be continuing my studies at Newbold. She has always been a tower of strength, always the rock behind me and the one who encouraged me and propelled me forward, to go on to achieve and to strive by the grace of God to reach my goal. I could see that she was shattered and devastated. Like me, it brought tears to her eyes and we were both extremely disappointed. What would we say to the church? We had already announced to them that I was going to Newbold. Now I would have to make another announcement that I had dropped out, for a reason, which even I didn't understand.

Life goes on even when everything appears to be a challenge. Eventually, Marsha and I decided that since the rules of the Home Office state that I had to do a degree course, I would divert my attention to another degree. So, it was with a heavy heart that I enrolled in law school to do a law degree LLB to be precise. It felt like "The Incredible Dream" was now a nightmare.

12

Law School

I was now going to be enrolled in law school to do a law degree, knowing that I had started Newbold and not finished the access course. If I had been allowed to finish my access course, at least I could have taken that to do the law degree and started Year One but now I seemed to be stranded in the middle of nowhere. Should I go and begin another access course from scratch, or would they take me in half-way, since I had already done one semester? By now I was prepared to do anything and if I needed to do the access course from scratch, I would.

I'm not one who gives up easily and I know by the grace of God I would achieve what God wanted me to. The word of God says, what shall separate us from the love of God which is in Christ Jesus our Lord, shall tribulation or distress or famine or being dropped out of Newbold College are principalities, are powers, nothing shall be able to separate us from the love of God which is in Christ Jesus our Lord (Romans 8:38, 39).

At the beginning of law school, I said to Marsha that I wasn't sure what would happen but I was going with an open mind and open heart and whatever the case, I was resolved to start all over again from scratch. I wasn't going to give up. I told her it would be a long road to complete the law degree in four years, including the access year. I had a church sister, who was going to that same law school and we spoke about a law degree. She encouraged me to come there where she was currently in her second year.

I went to the law school one morning and presented myself at Admissions. I took my transcript from Newbold College and all that I had done in terms of studies, from my high school onwards and applied to be enrolled in the access course at the law school. I let them know that I had been enrolled last semester in another institution and I'm applying here. They looked at my transcript and said if this is what you got in your access course, then this is excellent! This is very good, we will take this, plus, you have other subjects that you have done already. This is sufficient, you can be booked straight into the degree program. There is no need for you to do the access because you're well qualified, they asserted. I was completely shocked! I was flabbergasted! How could my own college have turned me away, saying that this wasn't sufficient when I was now being accepted on a degree course at Holborn College accredited by the University of Wales? Newbold was also offering their own degree (BD) accredited by the University of Wales. The only difference being that theirs was in theology while the other was in law. If they were doing it for the money, they would have insisted I did the access course again from scratch and get an extra year's money from me. But no they were really honest; they told me I was more than qualified to do the law degree.

Again, I could see the handiwork of God in my life. I could now get on and do my degree. The word of God says that God is able to do more than all we ask, think of or imagine (Ephesians 3: 20). Indeed, God will not give you more than you can bear (1 Corinthians 10: 13). Evidently, "The Incredible Dream" was still alive so I gladly paid my money and enrolled into the law degree as a first-year student. In that first year, I would be doing English Legal Systems and Skills, Contract Law, Criminal Law and Constitutional Law, four heavy-duty studies.

I was determined not to miss a single class. I would make sure I was present at everything, even though I had to be working and financing myself and my wife was working as well, helping to finance me. It was going to be a challenging time.

I paid my money and went back home, happy to give my wife the good news that I was enrolled straight into the degree course and I was now a first-year law student. She was overjoyed, I could see the excitement in her face and she could hardly contain herself. She was so happy that God had vindicated our hard work and was turning things around for us, proving He was at work in our lives. As He declares, "I will never leave you nor forsake you when you pass through your waters, I will be with you, when you pass through the fire I will be with you, I will never leave you nor forsake you said the Lord of hosts (Isaiah 43:1-3).

I enrolled in my Law degree and completed my first year by the grace of God. Truly the Lord is amazing, He is wonderful, He is glorious and He will not give you more than you can manage. I had been down and He raised me up, so I can walk on the mountain, he raised me up. "The higher they build their walls, the higher I will jump. You can deny me; you can take my rights away from me but there's something inside of me so strong and you do me wrong so wrong" (Labi Siffre).

Not only did God bless us with the journey in first-year legal studies but he also blessed us with a new baby underway in that same year. Marsha came home one day and told me we might be expecting a baby and to confirm it, we got a home pregnancy test, which came out positive. Our previous baby had arrived five years ago, our daughter Rachel. This was a bittersweet experience since it would clearly be a greater challenge to finish my course with a young baby on the way. However, I studied harder and worked harder, pushing myself to the limit. I began to wonder if I should stop my legal studies and carry on with the baby, or should I do both simultaneously; it was indeed a challenging time for us as a family.

I remember going to a first scan in the Kings College Hospital. They scanned the baby to see if everything was OK. If there was a heartbeat and different things that they test for at six weeks and everything seemed to be fine. We thanked and praised God for His goodness and mercy and continued with our new baby growing inside my wife, while I was going to school and studying, my wife was also studying at the same time. After a short time, we realized that this pregnancy would be a challenging one. We needed to have God with us.

After 16 weeks, we went to see the gynaecologist, who told us that this baby was in trouble. By then we had moved to Lewisham Hospital since they had the history of our first daughter Rachel. I remember the doctor telling us that things weren't looking good at all and at 16 weeks pregnant there was nothing they could do. It was inevitable that my wife was going to have the baby today and that would mean it was far too young to survive. At 24 weeks maybe, or 28 more likely but certainly not at 16 weeks, there was no chance. They told us that unfortunately, we would lose this baby just like our first daughter.

They took us up to the ward and gave us a special bed, warning us that it was a matter of when and not if, we would be losing the baby. They tried to comfort us but I went into that room and broke down. I was crying so much and pleading with God. Like Jacob who wrestled with God (Genesis 32: 22-32), I was saying please Lord not now, not the second one. I was praying to God please, Lord help us. The enemy had taken our daughter Rachel, please Lord don't let him take our second daughter, from us as well. I was powerless to do anything, so I left everything in God's hands. When the children of Israel were backed up against the wall and Pharaoh and his army were behind them and on both sides were mountains and in front of them the Red Sea, it was at that time that God said to the children of Israel, Hallelujah! Fear not, stand still and see the salvation of the Lord, for the enemy that you see today you will not see again no more (Exodus 14: 13). It was with strong faith and tears that I cried in that ward, cried to God to encourage my wife at the same time. We were both crying and there was no-one there to comfort us but the word of the Lord.

God said, "Is not my word like a fire and a hammer that breaketh in pieces" (Jeremiah 23: 29). Yes, Lord, you did hammer your words through by saying you will never leave us (Matthew 28: 20). In difficult times you will always be there for us (Isaiah 43: 1- 3). God had proved Himself to be strong another time.

It was at this challenging time that I went to Lewisham Shopping Centre, my eyes welling up with tears and trying my best as a man not to cry in public, which I managed to do. Men are human beings with emotions and we should cry when we are hurting. I was in a shop buying clothes for the baby, tiny clothes because if the baby should come at that time she would be fully formed and we would need to have clothes for her. I also bought some clothes for my wife.

I got back to the hospital with tears and pain and sadness, talking to my wife, trying to assure her that God is still God and the Lord will still do something for us. We needed to have faith in God. We still needed to put God to the test because it's God who says "prove me now said the Lord of host and I see if I will not open the windows of heaven and pour you out a blessing that there will not be room enough to receive it" (Malachi 3: 8-11). We passed through that night and thank God the baby wasn't born. When they released my wife from the hospital, she was on total bed rest.

I was working and studying and I had to get up early and make sure I cooked enough food to keep her through the day. Breakfast, lunch and dinner were prepared. All my wife had to do was serve herself. I cleaned, washed and cooked. Then I washed the dishes to make sure everything was clean. We got to 20 weeks and my wife ended up in the hospital again; the doctor said she had a slim chance of surviving. She said she was sorry to be so blunt with us, but in her professional opinion, this baby would not survive because history always repeats itself.

I was sure our baby was going to live. We had gone 4 more weeks than the professionals said we would have a good chance and if God could have given us four weeks extra, He could give us another four and another four and another four. God will take us there and we will have the baby by God's grace. We spent another two weeks in the hospital and then returned home. The same routine followed and we kept going back to the hospital every single month. My wife was admitted to the hospital each time, either for one week or two. They got used to seeing her there.

Meanwhile, Brixton SDA Church got used to seeing me alone every single month. I told them that my wife was in the hospital again. Even today some people still ask me which one of the babies was it, that your wife was always in the hospital with? They all remembered it was a really tricky pregnancy for my wife. My church family would come and look for us and visit us at home. They gave my wife communion at home when I was an elder in Brixton Church.

Then finally one night, my wife and I were sleeping at home when she woke up and told me to call the ambulance. They took us to Kings College Hospital where she was admitted and this would be the final admission before the birth of the baby. Everything was done; we had bought everything for the baby, the clothes and my wife's bag was packed. The only thing I forgot was to bring the little camera I had at home. We had arrived at the hospital at about 4 or 5 in the morning and I asked the doctor if I could rush home and get the camera? We only lived 3 stops from the hospital and at least I would be able to take pictures of the baby. The doctor told me that now my wife had gone into labour, the baby could be here at any time now and if I wanted to witness the birth, I had better not leave now.

I stayed around and waited and waited and waited until the evening came and I had to go home and still there was no baby. They said they would call me back when the baby was on its way so I should make my way home and come back the following morning. I called work and let them know that my wife was in the hospital, so I wouldn't be back in yet. I took time off from work and spent Monday and Tuesday at the hospital. Still no baby, so they told me that before the morning was finished, they would have the baby. I came back on Wednesday as usual and my wife was there contracting but not having the baby, they weren't in any rush to get the baby out. They said each day was a plus for the baby anyway, so keep the baby in as much as possible because 40 weeks would be the ideal time for the birth.

That Wednesday night, I finally left my wife and went home. It was a hard thing for me to do. I told her, Honey, you are going to have a baby tonight. The midwife overheard me and said she had been a midwife for over 16 years and she was adamant, my wife was not going to have the baby that night and I should go home, get some rest and come back in the morning. They would still be here in the morning and she would not have the baby tonight. I said you know what, I'm sure my wife will have the baby tonight. I didn't like to challenge professional people like that because they know what they are talking about and it's based on their experience. But somehow the Lord was telling me that my wife was going to have the baby that night and it's better to obey God rather than men (Acts 5: 29).

So, I finally and reluctantly went home, telling my wife to keep her phone near her. It wasn't the fancy sort of mobile that people have today, but it was a phone anyway. I told her to keep it close to her and I would keep mine right by my bedside and I would be there as soon as possible.

I got home very late and cooked myself something to eat. Not ideal at that time of night but I was hungry so I cooked up some heavy food, with dumplings and stuff and decided I should stay up a little while before going to bed. Just after 23: 30 HRS, my phone rang and I picked it up immediately. It was my wife, she had gone into labour and they were rushing her to the theatre. I put my clothes on within seconds and dashed out of the house, running all the way from Brixton to Kings College Hospital. People must have wondered why was this man running at this time of night, minutes to 12?

Thank God I was physically fit. I ran all the way from my home, which was about three or four bus stops to Kings College Hospital. I ran straight in and up the stairs to the third floor. As soon as I got there, they told me that my wife had just gone into the theatre. I said OK thank you very much I'm going in to see her. But I couldn't go in without wearing any protective gear and it felt like ages before I was all ready and rushed into the theatre.

There were about 10 people in there with my wife; one midwife and the rest were doctors and nurses. The midwife was standing by my wife and they had everything ready to take the baby out because it was going to be a caesarean section, as they feared she was losing the baby. I know that Jesus is the same yesterday today and forever; Lord I know you will save us even at this point (Hebrews 13: 8). The doctor insisted he should perform the operation immediately, to save the baby at any cost and he was ready to cut and remove the baby.

Then the midwife turned to the doctors and begged them to give her another chance; she would watch and when it was ready, she would tell my wife to push. Then she said to me, please Sir, don't say anything because I was telling my wife to push but I was doing it at the wrong time. The midwife with her professional eyes would look and see when the contraction was coming and when the time was right to push and if she pushed at that time it was highly probable that the baby would be born naturally.

As difficult as it was to keep still and quiet in the best interest of my wife and the baby, I had to do it. Then the midwife looked at my wife and she saw a big contraction coming, and she told my wife to push. She made a big push and shortly after I heard the baby crying. Finally, Hannah had arrived, born in the middle of a crowd of people, she sounded excited and surprised to be here. It was now the morning of the 21st of June, the longest day of the year.

They invited us to stay over one night at the hospital with the baby to see how Mum and Dad would bond with her before taking her home, which we did. We had to feed our baby that night and to God be the glory, everything went well and we were allowed to take our daughter home the following day. These were exciting times indeed. At home, the cot and everything was ready for the baby and when we took her home, we were so excited. She was the prettiest baby, she was healthy and strong and we stayed with her until she grew and the rest, as they say, is history.

Life was challenging at this time but God was good to me. I was teaching Bible class at Brixton on Sabbath afternoons and Tuesday evenings. I was also leading out in Goodnews, a branch from Brixton as the elder there, where I was doing communion services, preaching and also in charge of the P.A, audio-visual system. What with having a young family and doing a law degree at the same time, plus working for a living, it was quite hard. However, I can say the hotter the battle, the sweeter the victory and the more challenging things were, the more grace I received from God for the journey (2 Corinthians 12: 9).

Looking back over my life and what God has wrought, I can say, I have confidence in the leading of the Lord. I can safely say we have nothing to fear for the future, except we should forget where the Lord has led us (Last Day Events p. 72. Ellen G White).

In these challenging times, both my wife and I were working and caring for our young baby. Sometimes, my wife would be doing the night shift at work, while I was on the day shift. Both of us were now juggling University studies as well because my wife had enrolled for a law degree from London University and I remained at the University of Wales. Most mornings we would meet each other halfway up the road with the baby. I would be going to university on the bus and my wife would be coming home on the same bus.

One day, my wife was getting off at the back of the bus and I climbed aboard, leaving the baby in her pushchair on the pavement. Everyone was looking around to see why this crazy man had left his baby behind only to see a strange lady getting off the bus and wheeling it away.

When I was going to University, I would be on the bus with the baby and head to the place where my wife was because most times we didn't even sleep together, one was at work and the other sleeping at home with the baby.

One day I got off the bus and left the baby on it. Again, everyone watched in astonishment wondering why he was leaving his baby on the bus and about to call the driver, when a lady got on, smiling from ear to ear. We exchanged a few quick words with me standing at the door, while she paid the driver, just to say "I love you" and "the baby's alright" and then to the relief of everyone they realised she was the mother and the baby was very happy and also smiling from ear to ear. Of course, at other times she'd be crying her head off because her dad had left her and her mum had taken over for the rest of the day.

There were days when I'd be leaving the house saying bye-bye to my wife standing with the baby in her arms who'd be screaming her head off:

"I want my daddy! Mummy, you go to work! Daddy don't go to work, daddy I love you, daddy!"

Then I'd kiss my baby and let her know that we were doing this for her and unfortunately, I had to go to work for her or I had to go to university to learn for her. We were doing it all for her. I used to leave home and on Saturday evening, after sunset

I'd do the night shift, staying at work all night, then doing a long day the following day, coming off work on Monday morning and making my way straight to University. After such a hard time at work and a long shift, I studied all day. Then I would return to work for an evening and night shift. The next day, Tuesday, I would make my way back to University again. Only after that would I have the privilege of going home to my young family.

Those were challenging times indeed for us but God gave us great strength and we never felt it was too much for us. We coped, we managed to endure. If we really couldn't juggle our time, we engaged a child-minder who was one of our church members at Brixton, to take care of her for us. At work, I'd be doing between 70 and 90 hours per week during the holidays. We had to pay international fees and had no recourse to public funds. Therefore, the school fees for both of us were extremely expensive. Between us, we had to pay a minimum of £5,000 per semester. Nevertheless, neither of us was kicked out of university because we could not pay the money. God always provided for us and we did not have any outside help to get that money. God was our helper as the psalmist says, I will look to the Hills from whence cometh my help, my help comes from the Lord who creates heaven and earth (Psalm 121:1, 2).

That's where we looked in difficult times and in times of need. We saw others dropping out of the university for a semester, or even a whole year because they were not able to find the fee but God always provided that for us. One day, I took my baby daughter to University with me, to pay some school fee over the holidays and I saw my Constitutional Law lecturer. He knew me quite well because I was always the one answering most of his questions in class. He asked if she was my baby and I said yes. He thought she was really beautiful and asked how on earth I managed to study with a young family. He didn't know I was a full-time elder at the church and running everything there, even without the pastor.

The pastor would allow me to be at the church, doing the preaching plan and everything. I was in charge of all the pastoral work, along with caring for a young family and studying for a law degree, full time. My wife was also working full time and doing a law degree. That lecturer said to me, this baby would become a constitutional lawyer and I smiled.

Finally, the hard work paid off. I finished my course in 2009 and graduated in 2010 with an Honours' Bachelor Degree in Laws. When I came to the end of my legal studies, the Company Law lecturer asked me:

"Have you got through with your PLC or with your BAR? Do you know where you will be going, to finish up your legal studies to become a barrister or solicitor?"

"I will be going to do theology," I replied.

She was disappointed; you could see the disappointment all over her face.

"Oh, Otis," she said. "You worked so hard for your degree. I know you as a hard worker and you have done so well in your degree. Are you going to throw it all away and not continue to be a lawyer? You would be a very good one."

I felt as if I had let her down. If I could, I would have changed from theological studies and continued with my legal studies because she was quite right. I had worked hard with a young family and working full time. It had been tough going, financially, emotionally and spiritually. I had been determined to finish my law degree and finish in fine style, to get a degree that would qualify me to go forward to be either a barrister and or a solicitor. God was so gracious to me; He helped me to get exactly that degree and now the choice was mine.

However, there was a calling on my life, which God had placed on me from the time I was approximately 7 years old. God placed it in my heart that I needed to be a minister of religion and I could not shake it off, no matter how difficult the times, I could not. I had taken different roads and done different things but I had to obey the calling because I could never be happy doing anything else except being a minister of the gospel. Undeniably, I would have earned a lot more by being a lawyer. I could be in a fine job in the city making thousands of pounds each year, but clearly, "The Incredible Dream" was overwhelming.

In my second year at University, I studied Public International Law (PIL). I did very well in the coursework and gained a First in the course work. I thanked God because I had worked hard for it. The day the results came out, I went to the office to see how I had done. I was praising God that I had received a First; in fact, I was the only one to achieve that with this particular course work. Then, with the paper in my hand confirming the result, I went into the Chancellor's office because I had real problems. It was now nearer to December and Christmas was imminent. I explained to her that I'm a Seventh-day Adventist Christian and I could not do anything secular on the Sabbath.

One of my exams, in Public International Law, the same paper that I had in my hand, was due on a Friday in January, starting at 2:00 and finishing at 5:15. Almost all our exams lasted three hours and 15 minutes. I asked her if she would kindly give me some form of lenience and let me start the exam a little earlier? I told her that the Year Manager was willing for me to do the exam in his office, with him in attendance. I would be doing it on the same day, so I wouldn't have the opportunity to tell the other students what was in the paper. I would finish my exam at about 3 o'clock which would be before the Sabbath and while the other students were in the middle of their exam. There would be no way for me to communicate with them during the exams. I would give up my phone and everything and not take a break at all unless if I had to but then the lecturer could follow me as protocol demanded.

I said that's the only way I could do the exams with a clean conscience. She asked to see my results and I handed her the paper. When she saw I had a First, she congratulated me. However, unfortunately, she wouldn't do anything to help me. She said after doing so well with the course work, it would be a great shame if I couldn't sit the exam. She suggested I should speak to my pastor and request some exception to allow me to do the exam with the other students. I knew that the Sabbath was beyond me; it was beyond pastors and priests; it is a divine command. This made the situation even harder. If the exam wasn't on my favourite subject, it wouldn't be such a difficult decision but because Public International Law was one of my best law modules, it was more challenging for me.

I pleaded with her and told her that unfortunately, the priest could not give me that time. My role in the church was next to the priest so I was a leading person in it and I knew what the word of God says. No priest could grant me an exemption to break the Sabbath. However, like Mrs Thatcher, that lady was not for turning and I walked out of the office feeling deeply disappointed.

I spoke to my Head of Year who felt very disappointed for me as well. I spoke to my lecturer who was really sorry that the exam was on a Friday. He knew how hard I had worked to become the only student to gain a First in the course work. My only option was to sit the exam later with a re-sit group. However, re-sit students had their pass marks capped so I would have no chance of attaining a First in that exam. It did not matter to me whether I got a First or not, the main thing was to please God, my King (Acts 5: 29).

I told him respectfully that because of my faith as a Seventh-day Adventist Christian, I could not do exams on the Sabbath, which is from sunset on Friday evening to Saturday evening sunset, 24 hours as held in, (Genesis 1: 5; Isaiah 58: 13; Ezekiel 20: 12, 20 and Mark 2: 27, 8). If I should do the exams, I would breach the Sabbath by at least an hour. I had no choice but to agree to join a re-sit group. I knew there would be consequences but at least I could still pass the exam and by now, I just wanted to get through it, finish my legal studies and get on to do theology and fulfil "The Incredible Dream".

He told me he liked my faith and that as it happened, he lived next door to a Seventh-day Adventist Christian in his home village but he didn't know what we believed in. He respected the fact that I had stood up for my faith and my belief in God and asked if I would invite him the next time I was due to preach in the church? He said he had been moved by the fact I had so much to lose but still had not been willing to give up on the Sabbath and what I believed in (Acts 5: 29).

He wasn't the only lecturer who knew about it. I found out that there had been a discussion at the staff meeting about this student who had stood up for his faith and other lecturers, some who were Muslim, came to me and said how they appreciated what I had done. They knew me to be a good student who worked hard so for me to do that for my faith and my religion, it must mean a lot to me. Eventually, I successful did the exam with the re-sit group. I was pleased and gave God the praise and glory.

I went to Cardiff for my graduation ceremony at the University of Wales, in St David's Auditorium. A lot of people from Brixton Church and family members wanted to come to support me. I asked the University if they had pupils who were not able to attend the ceremony and if so, could I please have some extra tickets? When I told them I needed 30, they were really surprised and said I must be very popular because they'd never had that many requested before but all was agreed and I was told to collect the 30 tickets on the day of the graduation.

I remember 30 people following me from London to Cardiff. We arrived the night before, my wife and I and the little one, because I didn't want to be late for graduation. The next day, we went to the University of Wales and found the large, St David's Auditorium. When I got to the desk to pick up my tickets that morning, I gave the lady my name and she realised I was the one who had ordered 30 tickets, she called all her colleagues over to meet me. They said in the history of graduation at the University of Wales, they had never had anyone order so many tickets before and I must be very popular, particularly because all these people had driven here from London to see me graduate! I told them I was a Christian and an elder in the church, which had over a thousand members and if we could have had more tickets, even more people would have turned up, to God be the glory.

13

Theology and Becoming a Minister of Religion, 2010

It had always been my incredible dream to study Theology and be a minister of religion. Even after my first year at law school, I returned to Newbold College and showed the people at Academic Services just how much I had achieved, by the grace of God. I showed them my transcript and my grades, which were all really good. I told them I was willing to transfer all my credits and come and start BD from year one at the college. They thanked me but said, unfortunately, this was not possible. However, when I had finished my law degree, I could come back and do a license in Theology.

This made me all the more determined to work even harder and after safely gaining my law degree, by the grace of God in January 2010, I went back to Newbold and showed them my transcript, which qualified me for the program of licence in Theology. Most of the folks that I left there some three years ago said they were surprised to see me back. Finally, I signed up for my degree for my licence in Theology and paid my school fee, by the grace of God and started in January 2010. It was with mixed feelings that I went back to Newbold. An official in Academic Services asked me if I would like a letter to go to the Home Office but I declined, saying this wasn't necessary because my status had changed. I wasn't going there because I wanted any Home Office documents, I was going because it was my calling from God and I wanted to fulfil my calling as a minister and a preacher of righteousness.

One of the lecturers knew my journey, he knew my pain and he was always supportive of me. He was delighted to see me back at Newbold, fulfilling my dream and my vision, since he was one of my lecturers on the access course that I did. When I went back there, God was great. I successfully passed by God's grace and was ready for graduation the following year.

My Law degree turned out to be very fruitful indeed, given the fact that Hannah was born at the beginning and Abigail at the end. To God be the glory great things He has done. As a result of my studies at Newbold College, I had to do a placement at a church and the placement officer informed me that I could do this at Greenwich and Battersea. I remember saying my goodbyes in February 2010 to the Goodnews and Brixton Seventh-day Adventist Churches, telling them that as part of the fulfilment of my theological studies at Newbold College, I would have to do a placement at Greenwich and Battersea for a full six months. As it turned out, I ended up staying on for the entire year.

On Monday the 22nd February 2010, my wife, who was pregnant, worked that night. By the time she got home, I would be starting work at 10 o'clock that morning so I went off and left her with Hannah. I was working on outreach and on my way to see my brother Albeno. I took the 177 bus, it was an ordinary day like any other, then out of the blue I received a call from my wife, telling me to come back quickly, she was going into labour. I told her immediately I was on my way. I pushed the bell to get off the bus and jumped off at my University stop, crossed the road and took the first bus coming back on the way to Kings College Hospital where the ambulance had taken her and

Hannah.

Della, my good friend decided she would take care of Hannah for the night and my brother Roxroy came and picked her up and took her to Della's house. My wife was in labour early in the morning of the 23rd and she gave birth to our third baby girl. A really difficult time followed because my precious new daughter was kept in the hospital and our faith was severely tried. Finally, I told the doctor that this weekend my daughter would be coming out of hospital. However, the doctor said that based on his professional experience, there was no way she would be leaving at that time but I stayed adamant it would happen.

That doctor told me I was putting my God to the test in the same way that he was putting his professional ability to the test. He came to me on the Friday and said he didn't like bet against me because he wanted my daughter to do well and come out of the hospital but she would not be released on that weekend. I told him today was just the beginning of the weekend, we had Saturday and Sunday left, so let's wait and see by the grace of God and he smiled probably thinking I like your faith, I like your optimism, I like what you're doing for your daughter but medically this is not possible.

So that Friday night, nothing changed. The following day the Sabbath, it seemed as if God was preparing a miracle for us. The baby was transformed altogether; no-one could believe she was the same baby. The doctor said they would continue to watch her for the rest of this evening and if her progress continued, she could come out on Sunday. She did so well, that is what happened. The doctors and nurses all came by. They said they had seen us always praying for the baby. Every time we came, I was reading the scriptures to her. They'd seen other babies who weren't as ill as ours, who didn't recover that quickly and they were convinced that God had answered our prayers.

All our medical team knew about the challenge I made to the consultant. When he was leaving that Friday evening, saying that our baby was still not well enough to go home, that's when I challenged him. Later, they came to see me, one by one, giving God the glory, giving God the praise, so the doctors the nurses and the clinicians knew that man's extremity was God's opportunity to work on behalf of His people.

In 2011, I travelled from London to Wales for another graduation, my second in two years, by the grace of God. The first one in 2010 was the degree in Law. Now, in summer of 2011, it was my wife and two daughters and I travelling to Wales. As with the first time, we spent the entire night down there.

I remember both babies walking around in the hotel where we were staying especially the new baby who was only just out of her home environment. We explored the entire place, walking around everywhere. I needed to get ready for the graduation the following day and went off to check where everything was. The children started crying as soon as I left. I thought it was worth checking because my wife now had two babies to look after.

They looked so pretty in their new dresses especially for the graduation, they looked just like twins. They sat with their mother as I stepped up when my name was called. I could see the people beside them smile when they shouted Daddy! I remember giving God the praise and glory because "The Incredible Dream" was grasped.

This was the place I wanted to be since I was a little boy. The Law degree had just been a stepping-stone to where I felt that God had finally wanted His servant to achieve and what only

God could achieve through me. All my life I had wanted to do Theology; I wanted to be a full-time minister of the religion and now I was graduating with honours by the grace of God. I see something here like this and give God praise and honour that my goal was fulfilled.

Also, six months into my Masters in Theology everything went according to plan, by the grace of God, after many years of struggle and disappointment, God finally stepped through. Whoever you are, if you have your dreams and you believe you can't attain them, just hold on to God and He will help you to achieve your dream even if it appears to be an incredible dream. It may be delayed but it will come to pass. God will not give you more than you can bear and even when you are going through it. He will make a way of escape for you, so you can endure (1 Corinthians 10: 13). He is the same yesterday, today and forevermore; God will always be there for you, He will always be with you (Hebrews 13: 5).

I know some people believe that life is against them and indeed this may have been so. You've been dealt a wrong card or a bad hand and you believe you will end up losing. I came to Newbold back in 2005, only to be disappointed and told to leave in shame, unable to fulfil my dream, "The Incredible Dream". But did I give up? No, I was determined by the grace of God to fulfil the dream that God has planted in my heart. God had called me to the ministry and I was going to be employed in ministry come hell or high water. I was tenacious, I was willing to go faster, to dig deeper and to press harder until finally, by the grace of God, I succeeded after much blood, sweat and tears. So, God will always be with you and will give you the strength that you need, if you want it bad enough, if you are willing to work hard enough and to pray long enough if you are willing to be guided by God enough, then surely He will help you to achieve your dream. God says higher than the highest human thoughts can reach, is God's ideal for his children, godliness (Desire of Ages p. 311).

The happiest place on earth for me is where God wants me to be. I could have graduated from Bar school, like my friends and colleagues I did my law degree with but instead, I was graduating in Theology. The call of God on my life was not to be a barrister, but a Theologian. At least at this time that's God's calling, if He is willing to change, I'm willing to go with Him. So, "The Incredible Dream" was finally realized.

When I came to the United Kingdom, I pledged to myself that I would do Theology and that's what I finally achieved by God's grace. I remember travelling down to London, resting on the Sabbath or at least the family rested because I was feeling fine. It had been a long day travelling from Wales and the following day, Sunday would be my graduation at Newbold. I sat there at Newbold, taking pictures, preparing myself for graduation. The photo on the back cover of this book attests to this. By the grace of God, it was a great event.

Newbold College is an institution divinely ordained to teach people Theology and to love God and His word. I had finally acquired the relevant credits to be graduated and I was pleased to know that I would be following the leading of the Lord in my life. Indeed, God said you shall be the head and not the tail, you shall have to lend and you shall not need to borrow (Deuteronomy 28:13). I graduated from Newbold by the grace of God and not owing one penny, despite all the difficult circumstances, the hard work and the pain.

I thank God for all the good Samaritans who helped me out

while I was at Newbold. There was a sense of achievement and accomplishment of what I had set out to do. It certainly hadn't been easy; it was difficult and it was tricky but God was with me all the way. He said I will never leave you nor forsake you (Isaiah 43: 1-3). I'm sure there are those of you out there who are experiencing difficulties and you might have had a rough start in life but God can see you through; He can do for you more than you can ever ask or think (Ephesians 3: 20). Just be determined to achieve by God's grace what you want to achieve; just have this can-do spirit and believe you can achieve all things through Christ who strengthens you (Philippians 4: 13). But if you have a negative spirit towards life and believe that life has thrown you a rough hand and you can't do anything with it, you will not achieve anything. Once you are determined to reach and achieve by the grace of God, He will obtain and achieve through you and He will get the glory, not you, because He is the one who gives you the will to accomplish and succeed, by His grace and His power.

Look at my background and where I came from, a little district and a small community in Saint Elizabeth which most people might not even have heard of: Little Bridge District. Most people might not have known my family; we were neither the bravest nor the brightest in the community, we certainly weren't the richest. I have never looked down on my family and myself because I have never thought of myself as someone who couldn't succeed.

I graduated from high school 20 years ago, to the day that I was now graduating with my degree, License in Theology. I never gave up on my dream. As the years went on, a lesser person might have given up but I knew that I could achieve it by God's grace. "The Incredible Dream" had materialized.

14

The Burglary That Changed Our Lives

2011 turned out to be a very difficult year for my family and me. I graduated from college in July and felt wonderful for accepting the call of God. I was working in Bethnal Green at the time and on finishing my graduation, I wanted to spend time with my family but I was going to work, coming home from work, spending the entire summer holiday working full time.

One day I had done an early shift and came home so that my wife could leave to work her next shift. I got off at Brixton and set off for home via the Brixton market area and down Coldharbour Lane where they were celebrating Jamaica's Independence Day, August 2011. I was very tired as a result of the work, so I went home, took a nice shower and had my dinner. My wife went off to work, she was still doing nights and I was left there with the two babies.

Eventually, I put the babies to bed and went to bed myself. We were all asleep when at about two in the morning I heard a knock on the door. Knock is an understatement, I heard a loud banging on the door and someone shouting: "Police, police!" I jumped out of bed wondering why the police would be kicking off my door; I then thought it's a mistaken identity because I hadn't done anything wrong at all. I had just graduated with my degree, three weeks earlier and now I was here with my children while my wife was at work. Why would the police be knocking my door off?

I got to the bedroom door and looked right into the

passageway. Then I saw the door literally flying across the passage into the hallway, smashing into the wall beside the bathroom and kitchen. Immediately, about 10 guys ran into my house wearing hoodies, still shouting that they were the police. I quickly realized that it wasn't the police, but my neighbours, hearing that would think the police were at my door and therefore wouldn't bother calling them. They came into my room where my babies were sleeping and demanded to know where the money was. I said I hadn't got any money. Then they kept mentioning a person's name that I had never heard of, insisting he told them I was the one with the money.

"I don't know what you're talking about," I said, whispering. "I've got my two babies sleeping in the room and I wouldn't like them to wake up."

"Ok," said one of them. "Don't do anything to him in front of the children. Let's take him in the next room."

When I heard that, I realized that these guys were about to hurt me and yet somehow there was some sympathy there because when I mentioned the children, or the babies were sleeping. I thought to myself, OK I'm going in the room where the babies are because if they're not going to hurt the children then that's the room I need to be in because they're not going to hurt me either in front of the children.

When they saw the babies sleeping, they started whispering. We were all whispering! I was whispering that I hadn't got any money at all and it was a case of mistaken identity.

"You've got the wrong person here, I insisted, it's not me I'm a Christian, I preach at the church in Brixton. I'm one of the leaders in the church in the Brixton Seventh-day Adventist Church. So, I'm not someone who has got money at all. I just came home from work today and right now my wife is at work and so I'm home with the two babies."

One of them picked up my kitchen knife and then they saw my phone on the floor. I had two phones at the time and they took the smartphone. The guy took it right in front of my eyes and put it in his pocket. I didn't say anything at all because I knew the enemy was at work. He took it, pushed it in his pocket and then he moved on. I kept telling them I wasn't the guy they were looking for; they had mistaken me for someone else entirely.

That was indeed a frightening experience. Finally, they ran out of my house and kicked down my neighbour's door upstairs and proceeded to rob him. He told me in the morning that he was the one they were trying to find. I heard them running back downstairs after they robbed him and they kept running. God had protected me (Psalm 91; 46 & 23).

I eventually called the police and told them I had just been burgled. They said haven't you been watching the TV? I said no. There had been a big riot and burglary all over London. He said to me it's not only you. I said well my door is broken in two and it came off completely and I've got young babies at home. It was very cold at the time and the wind was blowing through the house. They told me there was nothing they could do. The best they could offer would be to send someone round within 12 hours, so about 2 pm tomorrow. They were overstretched as it was.

Reluctantly I hung up the phone. I wasn't going to get any help from them tonight, to fix my door. Not one of my neighbours came out, even to ask how I was. They were all too afraid to do anything; no-one wanted to say anything. So, I mustered all the strength I could find and managed to lift the door up and wedged it against the frame. The cold was still coming in but at least it was an improvement. The children slept like babies throughout this whole ordeal. I had prayed for them not to see what happened; I didn't want it to scar them for life.

I went back and looked in at the babies; they were still sleeping soundly and I praised God and thanked Him for His grace and goodness. I knew there was nothing I could do until the following day and if they decided to come back, I was at their mercy. However, thank God, they didn't return. They were obviously opportunists, preying on defenceless people. Crimes like this were going on all over London. I was just another unfortunate victim.

The babies slept on until the morning. Hannah was four years old at the time and clearly understood a lot more. When she saw the door, she asked me what had happened. I told her something went on in the night, which ended in the door being broken. I assured her all was well and I had called the landlord to come and get it fixed, which they did.

At about 5 pm the following day, the police arrived, 15 hours after the burglary. They said to us that if they found these people, I would have to leave the area, otherwise, they might come back for revenge. I had a young family and didn't want to be a party to any of this. Within two weeks, we had moved house. I never found out if they captured those guys and I didn't wait to get my phone back. We left and went to live in another part of London, far from that place. I just wanted my family to be safe and it was a long time before I could feel calm about someone knocking on the door, however innocently. My heart would start pounding, wondering if someone was coming to break into the house again. I had felt so close to death and knew that they could have killed me. Yes, it was mistaken identity but they could have wanted the person dead. There were 10 of them and they could have killed me easily. I imagined myself laying there, a lifeless body on the floor and my babies waking up finding me there, calling out for their daddy. Truly, the angels of the Lord encamp round about them that fear Him and deliver them (Psalm 34: 8).

All of this had happened just three weeks after my graduation. It was an experience I would not wish on my worst enemies. At the time, the phone that the burglars left me with wasn't able to make calls, so I used the landline to call my wife was at work. She was very surprised I had called her at work. Anyway, she couldn't speak at the time so she told them that she'd call me back shortly on my mobile. She didn't know what had happened, I no longer had a mobile. When she left the house, all had been well and as normal. She assumed it was a safe place because we had never been burgled before. We were married in Jamaica for four years and never by the grace of God been burgled. We had lived safely in the UK for nearly a decade so now she thought everything was OK. I waited and waited because I knew she wouldn't be able to call me. Then I called her back again and told her what had happened. Now she was scared to death and when she arrived home, she could not believe her eyes.

I had a driving lesson that morning and the instructor had been calling my phone, telling me to come down because he was outside. Of course, I didn't get any call. When he came to my door, he realized what had happened. I told him I didn't have a phone anymore and also, unfortunately, I had to cancel my driving lesson for today.

I called my workplace and informed them of the horrible

event that had just taken place. I let them know that I was still without a front door so I would not be able to come to work that day. The manager said she was sorry to hear what happened; however, she needed me to come in anyway. I couldn't leave my house wide open after already having been burgled once but she kept insisting I should come in and to do my shift.

I did not leave my house; I would not leave my house in that condition and go to work. How could I work anyway? That was a terrible response from my manager and one she should be ashamed of.

15

British Citizenship

In 2012, I was granted indefinite leave to remain in the United Kingdom. I was so grateful to know that all my hard work, dedication and commitment to God had been rewarded. I really love the United Kingdom and have worked here to help to build this country. My grandparents came here in the early 60s and they too worked hard for the same reason. I'm happy to be playing my part here and this was a blessing for us as a family.

The following year more blessings came when I was also granted British nationality. I was now not only a citizen of Jamaica, the land of my birth, but I was also a British national. I am so pleased to be a citizen of both these great nations and it is something that I wear with enormous pride.

In June 2012, we were expecting our third child. The pregnancy was going well, everything went well by the grace of God with no apparent complications. When the time came for the baby to be born, I was at Newbold doing my Master's course and also very busy in the church. I was volunteering as an associate pastor at Plumstead Seventh-day Adventist Church for a whole year, while I finished my degree.

With the time getting near for the baby to arrive, I asked a church sister if she could be at our house to help my wife throughout the whole process. So that when my wife went into labour, for instance, she would be there to look after our two other children while I went with my wife to the hospital. The very night the sister arrived at our house, it all started to happen.

At about midnight, my wife rolled over in bed and told me her waters had broken and she was in labour. I rubbed the sleep out of my eyes; rushed to wake the lady and told her that my wife and I were leaving for the hospital straight away. I grabbed my wife's bag, helped her down to the car and drove off quickly. These were anxious moments indeed and I kept wondering what I would do if the baby decided to arrive in the car. I'm not a trained midwife neither am I the son of a midwife.

I headed quickly towards the Darent Valley Hospital. As I got to the top of the road, coming from West Street, I saw another car coming out of the intersection. I had the right of way and also, I had my wife in the car expecting a baby any minute. Usually, I'm a very polite driver and let people go in front of me, but not today. Then we came up to a roundabout after which was the massive traffic lights, just as it changed to green, I had the momentum so I shot ahead of the other vehicles waiting in line.

Suddenly, I heard the shriek of a police siren behind me. I wondered what was happening and thought there must be some emergency. It was an unmarked police car, with two white police officers inside and maybe they assumed that as a black person driving at this time of the night, I was up to no good because they pulled me over. I jumped out of the car and explained that my wife was in labour and I needed to get her to the hospital ASAP.

"I'm not sure what time my wife is going to have the baby," I said. "But she's in pain."

"Unfortunately," said one of the officers. "There is a mark on the car plus we have to check your status to see whether you are legal or illegal in the country. We have to check whether you have a licence to drive or not and we have to see if there are any points on your licence. We also need to know if this car is insured, or if it is stolen. So, unfortunately, you will not be allowed to go, until we have checked out everything."

Meanwhile, my wife was in the car, crying with pain. I could not believe those officers were really going to hold me until my wife started to have our baby right there in the car. I didn't want them helping me to deliver her. This stop was completely uncalled-for. I was driving within the speed limit otherwise for sure they would have charged me with speeding.

I felt that I had been stopped because I was black, young and driving at that time of night, in a mainly white community. I felt so disappointed, given the circumstances that my wife was in the car crying about the baby and they decided to check all of these things out. I wondered where was the human dignity? All dignity had gone from these men and they behaved worse than animals.

I can still hear them calling immigration, giving my name which was on my driving licence and asking if I was legal. Thank God, I have never been illegal in the UK or anywhere else not even for a day. I had indefinite leave to remain, so there was no problem. Next, they checked out my insurance and found that was OK. They checked if there were any points on my licence and it was clean. They did everything possible to hold us up.

"Ok," he said eventually. "There's no problem with you. Therefore, you are free to go."

I continued on my way, angry but driving nervously, not only because of my wife but because I didn't know if there would be another set of the police officers, waiting to stop me again, trying to delay us getting to the hospital safely. Neither my wife nor myself have ever been in any trouble with the law. We have lived our lives above the law, by the grace of God.

I was so relieved when we reached the hospital safely and I got my wife to the right department. I had my laptop with us, playing music and songs that she loved, to help soothe her. She was really in some serious pain by 5 o'clock that morning. The main nurse took a break, leaving us with a student nurse in her place. When the student nurse popped out for a moment, my wife was in serious pain and I realised the baby was coming at any moment. I couldn't find anyone so I pushed the emergency bell and the student nurse came running. I remember her literally holding the head of the baby trying to push it back in because she was so confused and had never delivered a baby before. I just kept pushing the bell until the nurses and an experienced midwife turned up and they finally delivered the baby.

I was so happy when I heard the baby crying and I was given the privilege of cleaning her, dressing her and staying with her for the rest of the morning. Then I made my way home to see the other girls who were crying their heads off, wanting their daddy to come back. The following day I returned to the hospital to collect my wife and another new baby. Before we left, I made sure the doctors knew to make all the proper tests and checks, to see that all was well with the baby.

16

USA and Jamaica

In August 2013, I flew to New York and met my dad. I hadn't seen him for over a decade and it was quite strange at first, for both of us. He drove me all the way down to Boston MA where I would be staying with auntie Cherry. It was a long journey, stopping on the way to get different things and then getting lost by missing our turning but we got there eventually and it was a great homecoming. Auntie Lucia from Florida had come down to see me; my cousin Sandra from North Carolina whose daughter was living locally. Randolph my uncle and his son Randolph Junior, my Auntie Vivienne and cousins Courtney, Judy were all local.

This was my first time in America and after we touched down at JFK and went outside, I could hear the car horns tooting loudly which reminded me of Jamaica. I reckon that America is not much different from Jamaica but in the UK, people don't use their horns so much. Also, it felt different driving on the right as opposed to the left. It felt like everyone there was driving on the wrong side of the road and it was quite scary for a while.

I spent two weeks with my auntie and also travelled back and forth a few times with my father. I enjoyed my time in America and the first thing I did was to look for things to buy for my wife and three daughters back in the UK.

Just before I left America, I went back to Queens NY and stayed with a cousin Anne. While I was there, I visited the huge shopping centre on Jamaica Avenue. I bought so many things for my family, clothes for the girls and so on, I needed to buy an extra suitcase to carry it all home in. My cousin that I was staying with was very busy working as a nurse and didn't have time to show me around Queens; however, we went to Jamaica Avenue once, after which I was on my own. It was so exciting, I felt really comfortable in New York buying gifts and walking everywhere on my own. It was a great experience. Since that time, I have returned to the States 7 or 8 times. I really love America.

When the plane touched down safely at Heathrow Airport, I gave thanks to God and made my way home to see my family. I had missed them all so much. I had only been away for two and a half weeks but it felt more like two and a half years and I had never left them before to go to another country, so it was very tough for all parties concerned.

My next big trip was back home to Jamaica for the first time, after nearly 12 years of living in the United Kingdom. Only this time it wasn't just me going on the journey of a lifetime and having a big adventure, I was going back with my wife and three children. It was a totally different experience. We did a lot of shopping in preparation for the trip, thinking about what food we should take and probably got a lot of unnecessary things.

Getting on the plane with three children, aged one and a half, nearly 4 and 6, who had never flown before in their lives, was quite an experience but we enjoyed the journey. When we landed in Montego Bay, we could feel the heat as soon as we stepped off the aeroplane. Even though it was November and supposed to be a bit cooler, it was so hot it was unbelievable. We made our way to immigration control and answered questions about how long we were staying. Because I had travelled on my British passport, they questioned me even more. I realised then that I should have gone on my Jamaican passport and come back on my British one. So, the whole process took longer and the baby was very miserable and crying for us to hold her. It had been a very long journey.

My cousin Richard and my wife's bother Garfield were there to transport us to St Elizabeth while my wife's mother Mrs Betty, Sisters Alicia and Debbie met us at the airport. We had 10 suitcases, which couldn't all fit in the cars with the passengers as well. We were so excited to see each other; we then travelled to Saint Elizabeth, which was nearly 70 miles from Montego Bay.

I must admit, I found it a bit scary driving through Montego Bay market, with all our suitcases visible in the back and everyone knowing we must have come from abroad. There were so many things said about the dangers in Jamaica since we left admittedly, I was a bit worried. However, it wasn't as bad as we thought because we passed through there quite easily.

The next hurdle we encountered was going down from the top of Saint Elizabeth to Maggoty and on down to Middle Quarters. A big party (dance hall) was in full swing and it wasn't yet dark so everyone could see our suitcases hanging out the back of the car. Some people were saying the foreigners are coming down; the foreigners are here with the suitcases in the back. We were terrified to death but thank God even then everything was ok and we got to the hotel safely.

It turned out to be a difficult night.

"Daddy, can we go home now please?" said my second daughter, Abigail, just as we were getting ready to go to bed.

"Unfortunately, sweetie this is going to be home for the next six weeks," I replied as gently as I could.

It was our first journey and we had booked for six weeks. Can you believe that? Not for two weeks or three, but six and we were going to be in Jamaica for all that time. It was incredibly hot and the air conditioning didn't appear to work.

Of course, very soon we started having a great time in Jamaica. We enjoyed eating delicious fruits and lovely food; it was fabulous for our first trip there as a family. I would recommend it to anyone to go to Jamaica and visit as often as you can because it's not as bad as some people say it is. Jamaica is still a lovely place, a beautiful place and great people, with wonderful spirit and attitude. Also, the beaches are out of this world.

When I went back to my own community, I hardly recognised anything. It all looked completely different from the place I had grown up in. It still had a raw beauty about it and I loved the freshness and purity. It had none of the pollution of London and as soon as we arrived my hay fever disappeared and I was breathing in pure air, it felt great.

17

Full Employment

By 2014, I was back at Brixton as an elder. After finishing two campaigns in both Welling and Tottenham we went to Jamaica and returned at the end of December 2013 just days before the New Year began. So, in the New Year, we were going to Brixton Church where I was still serving as an elder and would remain so for the next two years at least.

One day, I saw Pastor Philip who called me over and said some folks had seen a campaign I did in Welling and they were requesting that I come to serve with him as a pastor there. At that time, I wasn't working as a pastor in Brixton Church. I discussed this with my wife and a few of the elders and the pastor at the time. Then in March 2014, we moved to the Lewisham Seventh-day Adventist Church to serve as an associate pastor in a voluntary role.

I was still doing the night work in Bethnal Green and we were living in Catford by now. So, I would travel from Catford to Bethnal Green and then I would do my work. I volunteered there as an associate pastor, working hard for two years. I was also heavily involved in missionary work. I've always enjoyed winning people to the Lord and baptizing people into the Kingdom of God. Sometimes I would do campaigns. I would baptize people and stay at the campaign all day and then I had to go to work all night. It was hard going.

Perhaps the toughest one I had was when I baptized 16 people on my own one Sabbath evening. I finished at about 8 o'clock then had to get to work by 9:45 pm in Bethnal Green. I just had enough time to drop my family home in Catford, change quickly and get to work on time in Bethnal Green. To say I felt tired that night would be an understatement but God gave me strength and the following day I was back to work again. Sometimes I would leave from board meetings in the night and go straight to work. It was tough but God always gave me the strength that I needed. At the end of two years of volunteer work in Lewisham Church, I was picked up. In other words, I was now employed by the church, which I really appreciated. Finally, I was employed to do the work that I really loved and I didn't have to go and do my night-work before coming back to do my day-work anymore.

We went back to Jamaica for our summer holiday in July 2015, my wife, our three children and me. We had a wonderful time. One day I was in my yard where I was born, near the guinep tree when I received a call. I looked on my phone and realized that it was Pastor Davis, President of the South England Conference. After exchanging platitudes, he informed me that he would like to pick me up after the conference session in September. I was so excited. I had waited for this for so many years. Finally, I was to be an employee of the church, not only that but I was to be employed as a pastor. I gladly accepted the call to ministry and let him know that as soon as I was back in the UK in early September, I would let him know and come into the office to touch base with him. Indeed, "The Incredible Dream" was materialised to the glory of God.

When I got back, he was so busy making plans for the conference session it was unbelievable. He told me I would not be staying in London but they were sending me to the country. It would be a great challenge for me. However, I was willing to do whatever God was calling me to. They wanted me to go to Bristol and serve as a pastor there in the Bristol district of churches. I was not opposed to it at all. However, it would be a great challenge because my wife was by now in her second year at university, studying nursing, with one more year to go and she was doing this in London. It would be difficult if not impossible for her to move all the way to Bristol. Nevertheless, I accepted the call and was willing and ready to make another set of sacrifices as a family.

Then Pastor Richard De Lisser was elected as President of the South England Conference. He called me to the office and spoke to me kindly about my family life and my current situation with my family and my wife. When I told him how difficult it would be for me to move at this particular time, he immediately decided not to send me outside London because that could be disastrous for the family and I had made so many sacrifices already. This made it possible for my wife to successfully complete her degree in Nursing as she did with her Law degree years earlier. She is thankful to God for the ability to finished two massive degrees in difficult circumstances. I was happy to continue at Lewisham and Downham where I had already served for nearly two years for free as a volunteer pastor.

I continued for the rest of 2015 when I was called and asked to move to a neighbouring district as the leading pastor without a supervisor, while someone else would be coming to my current one. That move turned out to be perfect for me. I didn't have to travel too far but most of all I had my independence, as opposed to working alongside another pastor. I loved my independence. I wanted to exercise my God-given gifts as opposed to always being in someone else's shadow. So, when I received the call from the conference, I was over the moon and gladly accepted it, grabbing the opportunity with both arms.

However, as the conversation continued, the administrator asked for my opinion on the person who would be exchanging place with me as an associate pastor. I had to be honest, based on what I knew about the district personally; I didn't think it would be the best thing at this particular time. In fact, I said I thought it would really affect the district in a negative way. As I said, I had really wanted to move to that other district but now I had to sacrifice my own wishes and stay where I was for the good of the church and to make sure, by God's grace that those churches had a solid foundation and would not get such a shaking at such a difficult time.

The administrator said how much he admired me. Here I was giving up my dream of going to a church on my own to stay longer in my current place, for the sole purpose of the church, not myself. I told him, to God be the glory, great things He has done. I loved my church and I had an honest heart to work for my church and see the best for it, even when it might not be the best for my family and me personally. It was indeed a hard decision but by God's grace, I was able to make it.

The opportunity to go out on my own eventually came about. The district I was posted to was Sydenham and Downham. I spent three wonderful years in Sydenham and in Downham, I did 5 glorious years. During this time, I had the privilege of baptising Hannah my daughter, which was very emotional. I had made a sacrifice but God gave it back to me in another way, to God be the glory, great things he has done. I did enjoy my time in both Sydenham and Downham.

18

The Twins

In early 2017, my wife said she thought she was expecting another baby. We did the test and double-checked, it was positive, so off we went to the doctor. At the appointment for the referral, the doctors congratulated us. We were expecting another baby and didn't know whether it was a boy or a girl. Our babies had all been born at Kings College Hospital, where we knew the midwife care to be excellent. However, this time the doctor said because it was early days, he would refer us to the clinic at our local Lewisham hospital, where we could have all the regular tests. For the six-week test however she referred us to Kings College.

So, we went to Lewisham for a normal clinic appointment and sat down in the triage area. As we got there, the nurses were calling people; it was like a walk-in clinic and people were going in and out the whole time. I noticed one young lady before she went in. Then when she came back out, she was so excited and kept calling people on her mobile: her partner, her mum, friends, everyone, to tell them all the amazing news, she was expecting twins. This was obviously a big surprise as well as an exciting one.

We sat there observing all this and smiling at the young lady. I turned to my wife and we went into a theoretical, light-hearted discussion of what would we do if we discovered we were expecting twins. Of course, we weren't, we were expecting one more baby. We fantasized about this while we waited our turn.

Eventually, the time came and we went in for our consultation and X-Ray ultrasound to see what was happening with the baby, if the baby was Ok, growing properly and so on.

After the test, the doctor sat down with us and we talked about having another child; we already had three, whom we loved and were quite happy to have a family that size. However, we were excited to be adding one more to our family.

"I know you were expecting a baby," she said. "But actually, when we did the scan, we didn't pick up a baby."

So, we looked back at her wondering what she was talking about.

"I'd like to let you know, there isn't one baby in your womb, there are two. You're expecting twins!"

We were completely shocked. We couldn't believe it. We had three children and now we were about to have five! I remember we sat down and tried to compose ourselves.

"Are they identical?" I asked. "Or is it too soon to know?"

"They are identical twin, yes," she replied, smiling.

I asked if having twins would be any different from having one baby and she said it would require totally different maternal care from what you would have normally if you were expecting a single baby.

I remember coming out of the clinic, thinking that's really tough for my wife and trying to digest the whole matter. How would we tell our children, first of all, and then the rest of our families? This was going to be a tricky time all round. However, we had time to think about it and compose ourselves on the way home and when we got there, we did what we had to do. I told them their Mum was carrying twins, which would be coming to join them. We didn't mention any of the concerns we had about possible problems giving birth to them, we kept the full story to ourselves and decided to trust God.

We attended special meetings for twins at Kings College hospital, every two weeks and checked to make sure the babies were growing properly, that one was not bigger than the other. There were so many things that could have gone wrong with our twins; we turned up fortnightly so if anything was wrong, they could just nip it in the bud by the grace of God.

Because they were sharing the same placenta, one baby could be consuming most of the food and the other getting nothing. If that were the case, they would have to perform an operation or procedure to help the other one to balance. One baby could be big and the other small. One could be unwell and the other one fine. They were ready to do operations on a list of things that could have gone wrong with the twins. We give God praise and glory and honour and power and Majesty and might for His kindness (Revelation 7:12; Jude 1: 25). I went with my wife to all the appointments. When the babies were roughly 2 ounces different in their growth the doctors said this was a good sign and by the grace of God there was no problem at all. We were eventually told he would have to do an elective caesarean, which meant the operation would be planned in advance and she would not have to go into labour. The date was set for 17th of August 2017.

I arranged that I would give the girls their breakfast that morning and then drop them off at cousin Sister Hilary's. She kindly offered to keep all three of them for us and have them to sleep there on that Thursday night. I got the children up early; they were really excited and looking forward to the whole thing.

Then I set off with Marsha and when we reached as far as Forest Hill, I asked her to call them just to assure them we were on our way. She phoned the clinic and said we would be there on time to prepare for the elective caesarean operation booked in for today. The lady sounded surprised and said there was nothing on the system about any C-section that day.

"I think you've got your wires crossed," she said finally.

I said to my wife there was no way we were turning around and going back home. We had made all these plans; I had taken time off work. This was definitely the date they had given us and it was their mistake, not ours. I told her we were going down there this morning and she was going to have the twins then by the grace of God. We had already told everyone at the church that we were going to have the babies today and I knew they were all praying for us. I had promised to keep them all posted about what was happening, through our WhatsApp group.

We finally arrived at the hospital and they repeated that there was nothing on the system to say my wife would be undergoing caesarean surgery today. However, I had all the paperwork to prove our case and I was able to tell them that it was their wires, which were crossed, rather than ours. We would wait here until someone kindly told us what time would be going into surgery, thank you very much.

Forced to admit that it was their fault, they agreed and we went into surgery at approximately 9 o'clock. I contacted everyone via the church WhatsApp and asked them to please pray extra hard for us because we didn't know how things would go from here on.

The medical team went straight to work preparing my wife for the operation, anaesthetising her body from the waist down, asking her if she could feel anything in all the different areas they targeted. When she assured them that she couldn't feel a thing, the surgeon arrived. They were all very kind to her and introduced themselves one by one. She told me afterwards that at that stage it felt like a very frightening experience altogether. She had given birth before of course, but this seemed like a much more dangerous procedure that they were going to perform. It was a first time for her and some people did not come out of it alive.

When the procedure started, they put up a shield, so she couldn't see what they were doing but she felt a lot of poking and poking and poking. She was just wondering when she was going to see her darling babies and then finally, after the pushing and pulling, they took out one baby and showed her to my wife. Then they cleaned the baby and brought her to me. I had been holding my wife's hand throughout but then I held the baby, while the second twin was born.

They put the babies in the cot and Marsha was transferred to the recovery unit, because she had gone through major surgery. She was doing well. Her blood pressure and all her vital signs were fine and we have to thank God for that. She saw that her babies were fine too and the doctors arrived to confirm that and congratulate us. She was kept in recovery for another couple hours of hours and then brought to the maternity unit.

The babies had done so well, they were ready to go home the same day. However, my wife had to recover in hospital from the surgery and of course, they stayed with her to get her breast milk. By Saturday, thank God, we came home with the two beautiful babies, they were absolutely gorgeous. It was unbelievable, we couldn't tell the difference between them at all. The only way we could know them was by their belly buttons.

When the umbilical cord was cut, one baby had one clip on it and the other had two. That's the only way we could tell the difference between Isabella and Gabriella, our two beautiful princesses. The girls were overjoyed to have their new, baby sisters at home with them and we all were hugely excited. The rest, as they say, is history.

I am so grateful to the Lord that He permitted me to be at the birth of our six children. I missed out on so much with my own father. He never went to any of my schools with me, on my first day or sports day. I would have loved to have him around but he was not there for me. He never went to church with me, nor even to the doctors. I have preached to thousands of people but he was never in the congregation. I had the privilege of graduating 5 times: High School; Law Degree; Licences in Theology, twice, one on Friday in Wales, the other on Sunday in England and a Masters in Theology and he has never been present at any of them.

Admittedly, my father and I enjoy a better relationship now that I am grown and independent and have achieved a lot by the grace of God. In light of my personal experience, I was determined to be there for my wife and children, to always do my best for then. I would strive to be there when they really needed me. I will always be there to support them in their high and low moments. Whatever our children become in life, I will always be there for them, because I love them endlessly. My wife has always been there for me, she is a tower of strength to me and it's not possible to measure the love I have for her. Above all, I pray for a long and healthy life so that I can be there for my wife and children and to see my children serve God by maintaining their own personal relationship with the Lord and finally to see my family in the kingdom of heaven.

My greatest achievement would be to influence my children, wife, family both biological and church family to be saved in the kingdom of God. As a pastor, it has to be God first, family next and then church family. Without God, there is no meaning but with God everything has a purpose. God has been more than a father to me but I still missed having an earthly father by my side.

19

New Home

By 2017, my wife and I had been trying for two years to get a house to call our own somewhere between Kent and London. Finally, my wife spotted a perfect one on the computer and we decided to go and view it. The lady was at home with her baby when we came. I really liked the house and it had a reasonable size back garden and it wasn't directly onto the main road. On top of this, the price came within our budget. We loved it so much we made an offer and thank God it was accepted.

Just after accepting our offer the couple that owned it informed us we would have to wait until they found their new house. We were stuck in a chain. That was not something we needed. It was now April and my wife was due to have the twins in August, plus the children were on school holiday in July and we had to have something that we could exchange contracts on in the next six weeks. Being stuck in a property chain meant we would have to wait until the owner found a property, then he would make an offer and then if that person was also in a chain, they would have to wait for them.

By the time we got to July, I told them we were withdrawing our offer; this had gone on too long. In fact, I gave them an ultimatum that if we were unable to exchange contracts before August, I would move on. I needed to know what my children would be doing for September and we had missed the entire summer holiday. Finally, the owner agreed that they would move in with their in-laws if they did not get a property by the

25th of August. This was very late for us clearly. However, since we'd been holding on for at least four months, we agreed.

I exchanged contracts on the 25th of August 2017, a week after the twins were born. That was indeed a blessing for us as a family, not only that we had our babies, but also God had now blessed us with our new home and we give God thanks for his goodness and his grace. Not only that, but God also blessed us with a brand-new car. The previous car we had was just big enough to carry five of us, that is my wife and I and our three children. Now the twins were here, it was no longer adequate.

God affirms that He would not give us more than we can bear but even when we are going through it, He will make a way of escape for us, that we can bear (1 Corinthians 10: 13). He is the God who supplies all our needs according to His riches in glory. Undoubtedly, my God shall supply all our needs according to His riches in glory by Christ Jesus our Lord (Philippians 4: 13 & 19). So, God provided us with a brand new, seven-seater people-carrier. We now knew we could take all seven of us around, safely and legally, in our family car, to God be the glory great things He has done indeed.

20

Ordination to The Gospel Ministry

After voluntary and paid roles for many years, I was delighted to receive a letter from Pastor Osei to attend an interview regarding ordination, at the conference session in September 2019. My wife and the twins and I made our way to the conference office in Watford. I did the interview and to God be the glory, it went fantastically well. I was told the wonderful news that I would be ordained at the end of the conference session. I was delighted, over the moon, thanks for His grace and His mercy; all those years of ministry had paid off. "The Incredible Dream" now had the cherry on the cake.

That was a special day indeed in our lives. I wished my mum had been there, to see what I had accomplished by the grace of God and by the support of my wife and children. Unfortunately, she's not around to see that all her hard work of sending me to Black River High School and instilling God in me had paid off. I have not been a perfect person but I pray that God will continue to give me the strength that I need to live for Him, no matter how difficult times are, I will be true to God and I'll be faithful to His calling on my life that I will live as an ordained minister of the gospel.

At the end of 2019, we completed our New Year service, where we had enjoyed a grand time and made our way home. We believed that this year, 2020 would be a year like any other, one day and one year nearer to the coming of Christ. No-one expected that the onset of the coronavirus, COVID-19 would become a pandemic across the entire world. It became clear that 2020 would not be a year of business as usual.

I remember the challenge of what we would do at church since everything had changed and no-one could hug or greet each other with a kiss anymore. The entire world was encouraged to take care, to keep a social distance from each person. It was indeed a time of trial and no-one knew how this pandemic would progress. The president of the conference made the announcement a week before the government would announce the lockdown, that all the Seventh-day Adventist Churches in the South England Conference would be closed as a result of the virus.

After closing the churches, we weren't sure what would happen next. As ministers, we started working from home and two weeks on, I was able to arrange our live-streaming service. I prayed to God about the series He wanted me to do and it was revealed to me that I should do the midnight series which was brand new and I had never done this anywhere before. It looked at the 10 Plagues in Egypt and then by extension, I would look at the Seven Last Plagues of Revelation 15 and 16. One closed off with Matthew 25 the midnight cry with the five wise and five foolish virgins who trimmed their lamps and went out to meet the bridegroom.

I had no idea that in the middle of this series, I would be placed on furlough, forcing me to stop immediately. We had audiences all over the world watching the meetings. I was furloughed for the month of May 2020. However, I was pleased to resume and finish the series in June, before being furloughed again in July. Furlough was a huge challenge for me, making me unable to communicate with and support my parishioners in the middle of a pandemic. Some of them were struggling and it was a hard thing for me not to communicate with them, to see how they were doing and to touch base with them. I was putting up daily devotional material on WhatsApp for the church group that I had created, trying to encourage people through the time of the pandemic, trying to walk through it together with my congregation. That was one of the toughest things that came out of being furloughed.

Some benefits came out of being furloughed, however. One was being able to spend more quality time with my family and doing things around the house and in the garden, planting my apple tree and a pear tree, strawberries, tomatoes and a whole range of other things. I also used the opportunity to fence off part of the back garden, for privacy and create a patio, something I had wanted to do for a long time. The icing on the cake during furlough was to use the month of May to write this book ("The Incredible Dream"), which I have wanted to do for many years.

21

Reflections on Ministry

If I were asked what were some of the challenges presented to me as a minister, I should say certainly being a pastor with one's own congregation gives unique challenges and opportunities. Being placed on my own in Sydenham and Downham was indeed a great privilege and a great honour for me personally. I had always wanted to go on my own and be independent as a pastor. The God-given talents and abilities that God has given to me, I wanted to put into practice as a pastor.

Going to Sydenham was quite a challenge. At Downham I had already been in charge of this congregation for two years; being completely new at Sydenham was different. They were just coming out of a great crisis, in which the church had split and they lost approximately half of their members. The church needed to be rebuilt and reunited, to work as a united force and a force for good in the community. This was a challenge indeed, to create unity and to bring people back together again in such a time of great challenge and great uncertainty.

I've always been a great believer in prayer and that with the power of God, prayer can move mountains. Prayer can do anything by the grace of God. I have never been one who is afraid of challenges. God has taught me through the years to be brave and to be bold but genuinely I'm a caring person; I love people and care about them. I want to see people being well; I'm not a person who will be rude to you neither should you be disrespectful to me because I will not allow it.

So, I went to Sydenham church and straight away prayed to God for His help to rebuild the congregation and indeed God was good to us. There was a good elder and some fantastic members at the time who were willing to push forward and for us to work together. When I started at the church, we had approximately 5 people left as board members, now we have 20, to God be the glory great things He has done. When I started there, the church had very few people coming out on a Sabbath but soon; the church was full and continued to be full. Sometimes we had so many people, particularly in our annual revivals, we couldn't fit them all and we had to hire the church, which we were permitted to do from time to time.

In the church, the membership went up and we increased the number of people we baptized, by the grace of God and many people transferred their membership to Sydenham church. Strong leaders transferred their membership and we had good reinforcement. I was leaving Sydenham church in good condition; the prayer meetings were back; other services were back and we held our board meetings every single month.

We had a plan at Sydenham to raise money to get our own church building in five years. Each year we would hold fund-raising concerts, which were free to attend. Then we would ask for donations towards our church building. Every Sabbath we would collect an offering for the church building fund and by the time I left, we had thousands of pounds by the grace of God and were well underway to get our own church building within the five-year deadline. God had been good; God has seen us through at Sydenham church, through the challenging times and now we were growing and developing by the grace of God and people wanted to be members there, because it had improved so much, God be the glory great things He has done. It was really difficult leaving Sydenham, we were really loved and appreciated there; we had a great time.

When I went there originally, to Downham, in 2014, I remember they had a small group of people worshipping in the smallest hall at the Wellesley Community Centre. After doing my first revival series, which became an annual event, people came from all over to support the series and we soon outgrew that small hall. In 2015, I encouraged the church to move to the biggest hall available for weekly hire, which we did. However, the parishioners there still had the mindset that we were just a little group. I inform them we should use the platform, which turned Downham into a proper church, and then the mindset of the people would change as well.

So, Downham began to grow and increased from approximately 20 people to 120 every single Sabbath, many people were baptized into the church, while others transferred their membership or became members through other ways. While I was at Downham church by the grace of God I helped them to change its status from being a branch Sabbath school to being a church. It became a new church in its own right, now known as Downham Seventh-day Adventist Church. After arranging everything, I invited Pastor McCormac from the conference to come down and lead our ceremony when it became a fully-fledged church and was welcomed into the sisterhood of churches at the conference session 2019, to God be the glory, great things He has done.

By the time I left the church, they had a proper building project going on, just like Sydenham. I had introduced a new building project and we raised thousands of pounds each year. We had fundraising events; people gave to the building program and it all went well. Downham was underway to having its own church building five years, by the grace of God.

Some people from another church challenged us and said if we should ever become a church, we would never be able to finance it, or at least the finances would be very low and soon we would have to run back to Lewisham church. However, I clearly remember telling the brethren that not by might, nor by power but by my spirit says the Lord of host, let us launch out into the deep (Zachariah 4: 6 & Luke 5: 4). And indeed, we did and God surprised us, not only did we have enough money to keep the church going, we were able to save thousands of pounds out of the income and paid all our bills and everything was covered by the grace of God.

Finance wasn't our problem at all; we were in the mission field, reaching out with our pathfinders. When I started at Downham church we had about seven children, including my own. When I left, we had nearly 50 children coming to the church each Sabbath, to God be the glory, great things He has done. I thank God for the leaders at Downham and the members. It was tough for us to leave that church, because my youngest daughter, Daniela, was just one year old when we started there. I was there from 2014 to 2018 December, so our children were quite young then and they knew Downham as their church and had many friends there. It was really difficult leaving Downham, we were really loved and appreciated there; we had a great time. So, it was tough for us to move and we did it with a heavy heart. We had to leave the district of Downham and Sydenham but God had been good to us, to God be the glory.

In 2018, we visited Jamaica as an entire family. The twins were almost one year old when we set out in August, first to visit relatives in Florida, my Auntie Consie, as she's affectionately called. While we were there, we had our 21st wedding anniversary, so after 20 years of marriage, we had been blessed with having twins. After visiting Auntie Consie, we went to Fort Lauderdale and stayed in the Holiday Inn Hotel. The children enjoyed it and we all had a great time. My Uncle Clenert came to see us there and treated us to a lovely meal. We also bought things to take with us to Jamaica.

Our flight down from the U.S took only an hour and a half. It was one of the reasons I should have liked to have lived in Florida. I loved the place and also it was just a short flight from there to Jamaica. When we landed, members of my wife's family greeted us. Then we took our rental car and drove to the hotel we booked, in Montego Bay where my wife's family accompanied us. The following Friday was the twins' first birthday and we felt so happy to celebrate it there in Jamaica. We had such a wonderful time, by the grace of God we thank God, and we praise Him for His love and His goodness.

Just before we left to come home, my wife's dad joined us. We were so pleased to see him and be able to spend some time with him. He brought lots of goodies for the children, so of course, they enjoyed themselves enormously as well.

Our flight back to the UK went via America and felt like a very long haul indeed. When we reached Philadelphia, the plane wasn't leaving again so we had to wait till the following morning, then the transfer was really tight but eventually, we got everything done, praise the Lord and landed safely back in the United Kingdom. I'd left our car at the airport car park, so we took the shuttle across to that and finally drove to our home.

By September of that year, 2018, I was in the middle of a campaign when we received the sad news that my wife's dad was seriously ill. We had only just seen him in August so this was a real shock. Then came the worst news that he had sadly passed away. We had been in Jamaica, as a whole family, for two weeks altogether and now we had to think about how to return there for his funeral. We discussed leaving Daniela, Abigail and Hannah here in the UK with someone looking after them and taking the twins with us, to go back and lay my father-in-law to rest. We have always been very close to our children and in the end, we couldn't bear the idea of leaving them behind, so we made the decision to take all of the children back with us, regardless of the cost.

So once again we flew down to Jamaica. I was the preacher at my wife's father's funeral and when I walked into the church and saw him lying there; it brought tears to my eyes. I was really moved; it was a tough time for all of us but God gave us the strength and finally, we lay him to rest, on Sunday the 28th of October 2018.

That night, we all returned to our hotel in Montego Bay to sleep. I'm an early riser, so the next morning I got up as usual at about 5 a.m. That's when I received a call from Pastor Osei back in the UK. He told me it was time for me to move churches and he was thinking of sending me to West Croydon District. At first, I thought of the distance; we had only moved house two years ago, from London to Kent where it was just a 40-minute journey to Downham and Sydenham churches. We assumed that after spending three years there, we would have at least another two years before leaving, taking us to 2021.

Anyway, he was asking me to move and it was hard for me; for a start, there was a really poor signal at that hotel and I had planned to go to Saint Elizabeth by myself that day, to carry out some business, after moving my family into another hotel in

Montego Bay. We had already spent time in Saint Elizabeth as a family, just two months previously, but I needed to return to my hometown, the place where I was born; I couldn't be in Jamaica without going to Saint Elizabeth, it would be impossible for me.

I discussed everything with my wife and then when I reached Saint Elizabeth, I called Pastor Osei and accepted the move to West Croydon and Pollards Hill churches. I told him God's will be done and if you want me to go there, I will go. My wife and I discussed the challenges facing West Croydon. They had some serious doctrinal issues there, which had split the church in two, and allegedly they were on the brink of being closed down. If that was to happen, the members would have to visit other Adventist churches.

I knew the problems I would be facing by going to this congregation; nevertheless, I have never been afraid of a challenge. Like Caleb I always say to God, Lord give me this mountain everyone else is afraid of and running away from and I shall go to it (Joshua 14: 12). If God is with me, I can go anywhere and I am not afraid of the challenges. Many people, when they learnt I was going to West Croydon district of churches, promised to pray for me. Some said it was unfair to send me there, they should be sending an older person with many more years' experience, maybe 30 to 40 years' experience in ministry to tackle the issues present there. Others warned me that this could damage my ministry, to go to a church with so many problems.

I accepted the challenge and went to West Croydon church. On my first Sabbath, I took my wife and children and we were introduced to the congregation from the pulpit. I said that I wanted to know nothing else among you except Jesus and Him crucifixion (1 Corinthians 2: 2). My intention was not to know about the problems, the divisions and who did what to whom, I was there to build the church, by the grace of God and to unify the church. That first day I informed them that I would unite the brethren, to make us a force to reckon with, by the grace of God. We would be a church again, by the grace of God.

I let them know that my intention was for evangelism, that I was an evangelist and I loved telling people about God, so we would be on the mission field, witnessing and telling people about the love of God. I also let them know that I was one who really loved end-time events and I would be preaching and teaching among other things on end-time events at the church.

So, it was indeed a great time for us at West Croydon. I started the church in January with a revival and the result of that was wonderful. People came up for baptism, we had our first baptism at the end of March where five precious souls were baptised and then in September, I did my first campaign in West Croydon. As a result of that, my own daughter, Abigail was baptized along with nine other precious people. We had our final baptism at the end of December and we had five people getting baptized. So, overall, we had 20 people baptized in our first year there by the grace of God.

Many people believed I wouldn't last the year there because the previous two pastors only spent a year between all of them but by the grace of God, we were able to finish the first year and the church had developed, it was growing, united and pushing forward. By the grace of God, we had achieved so much together. The brethren were loving, caring and kind. They even gave me a surprise party for my birthday in April, just barely 4 months in. It was a grand time, they had a massive cake and said: "We love you, pastor". Everyone told me that they had never done this for any other pastor in all of 35 years!

I was humbled by the whole experience and gave God praise for His glory and His goodness. For my family, and me the year continued going from strength to strength. In October, they held an appreciation day and we received gifts from the church. They were such a caring community of people and I felt blessed to be their pastor. God has been good indeed towards us. Admittedly the work brought its own challenges but God said I will be with you; I will never leave you nor forsake you (Hebrews 13: 5). And the members generally were extremely supportive and cooperative. They wanted to see their church do well by the grace of God. There may have been a few who would like to have their own way but God has always proven Himself to be good all the time.

Being on furlough and unable to contact my members was indeed a challenge. I thank God that I had the privilege of serving this church in the first year: to get air conditioning in the church; to get TV and live-streaming up and running and a food bank; we achieved so much it was unbelievable. We didn't spend our time fighting, even though some would have liked to continue as they had before. We used the time positively. This had to be our church. Unfortunately, after two years the conference kindly requested that I continue my ministry in the Peckham district of churches. The outpouring of love and affection from the members was overwhelming as the silent tears and audible outburst of grief flowed from the parishioners who really appreciate what God has done through my family and me.

This is my "Incredible Dream", the journey to be a Pastor. It proves that "I can do all things through Christ which strengtheneth me" (Philippians 4:13 KJV). I know that "my God shall supply all your need according to His riches in glory by Christ Jesus" (Philippians 4: 19). I could not have achieved it on my own; all the glory and praise belongs to the LORD. God has always guided me both in challenging and placid times. It demonstrates that whatever you set your mind to by the grace of God you can achieve. There should be no excuses based on one's birth, nationality, race, culture, ethnicity, disability and gender, excuses for not achieving is not acceptable. Evidently, with God on your side and a strong determination to succeed, you can do it. Be focused and don't be side-tracked. Please, stop making excuses; go forward and accomplish your "Incredible Dream".

The road can be difficult at times; honestly, sometimes it seems unattainable but with perseverance by the grace of God, if you keep pushing, keep pressing on, keep reaching forward, keep your eye single, keep looking at the prize (to accomplish "The Incredible Dream") then you can do it and you can make it by the grace of God. It's not by power nor by might but by my spirit said the Lord (Zachariah 4: 6).

I had this "Incredible Dream" since I was around 7 years old to be a minister of religion. Admittedly, many times I thought I would never reach my "Incredible Dream" consequently, I have taken many different parts but I could not resist it, neither could I be happy doing anything else except what God has called me to do. Note, to be a minister of religion is not merely a profession, it is a calling, it is a seed that God has planted in your life, something that you just can't shove off, something that you can't get rid of easily because it kept screaming in your ears. Undoubtedly, "Thine ears shall hear a word behind thee, saying, This is the way, walk ye in it, when ye turn to the right hand, and when ye turn to the left" (Isaiah 30:21). At times "The Incredible Dream" was very silent in my mind, it speaks quietly, it whispers, other times it shouts, it yells, it cries and roars, it would not leave me alone, it keeps calling me.

I thank God for the stable foundation that I was given by my mum. If it wasn't for my mum by the grace of God "The Incredible Dream" would not be accomplished to God be the glory. The biggest disappointment is that my mum died so young; hence, she didn't see the achievement. After my mum, God has blessed me with a dear, beloved, beautiful, sweet and incredible family. If it wasn't for my wife and children who motivated me, who pushed me and told me that I could do it, I would not have realized "The Incredible Dream". A big thank you to my wife, children and everyone else who have supported me.

I don't know what your "Incredible dream" is but I hope this book has inspired you to rekindle the fire and for you to go forward and accomplish "The Incredible Dream" that God has laid on your heart, with the assurance that if God could do it for me, then He can do it for you. Thank you very much for reading this book. God bless and keep you. Dear reader, if we don't get the chance to meet here on earth, please meet me in heaven by the grace of God, emphatically, that is ultimately "The Incredible Dream".

Acknowledgements

All praise, honour and glory go to the Lord since wisdom and knowledge derive from Him. I would also like to thank the human instrumentalities that played a part in the achievement of this book, *The Incredible Dream*. Thanks to my parents, especially my precious mother Ms Lizeth Evans (now deceased) who guided me spiritually and academically. Thanks to my loving wife Mrs Marsha Lewis who has been a tower of strength, her assistance is invaluable. Thanks to my daughters Hannah, Abigail, Daniela and twins Isabella and Gabriella who bore with me and supported me in the challenging times while writing this book, also my extended family, church family and friends.

About the Author

Pastor Otis Lewis' passion for pastoral ministry dates back over 30 years, however, it intensified within the past 23 years as an ordained elder. He began preaching during that time and has conducted many evangelistic campaigns, weeks of revival and weeks of prayer both nationally and internationally.

In 2010 he began a voluntary placement in Battersea and Greenwich. He continued this in 2012 in Plumstead. He was then employed by the South England Conference in 2015, and worked as an intern in the Lewisham and Downham district after serving for approximately 2 years as a voluntary pastor in Lewisham and Downham. He became pastor of the Sydenham and Downham congregations in January 2016, moving on in January 2019 to pastor the West Croydon and Pollards Hill churches. He has served as Secretary of Area 6B and currently serves as Area Youth Sponsor.

Otis obtained a License in Theology and a Masters in Pastoral Studies at Newbold College of Higher Education (University of Wales) in July 2011 and 2014 respectively, after completing an LLB Hons; Degree in Laws from the University of Wales.

He has been married for 23 years to Mrs Marsha Lewis, a nurse, and they have six children: Rachel (now sleeping in the Lord), Hannah, Abigail, Daniela, and twins, Isabella and Gabriella. He loves spending time with his family, enjoys swimming and exercise, travelling, listening to music, preaching and keeping abreast of current events.

Available worldwide from Amazon

---

www.mtp.agency

www.facebook.com/mtp.agency

@mtp_agency

Michael Terence
Publishing

Printed in Great Britain
by Amazon

33756128R00118